I am Duelling
With a River

Özkan Mert

I am Duelling
With a River

Özkan Mert

First Step
Publishing
Paving Ways For New Writers

First Published in USA in 2016 by First Step Publishing
Editorial / Sales / Marketing Office at
303-304 Garnet Nirmal Lifestyles Ph 2
Behind Nirmal Lifestyles Mall
LBS Marg Mulund West
Mumbai 400080
E-Mail:- info@firststepcorp.com
www.firststepcorp.com

ISBN: - 978-93-83306-36-7
Publisher and Managing Editor: Rohit Shetty
Branding, Marketing and Promotions by: Design Fishing
Digital Management by: First Step Corp
Typeset in Book Antique
Translator: Ender Gürol
Graphic Image: Ali Atmaca
Paperback: $ 15

About The Author

ÖZKAN MERT

Born October 21, 1944, in a two-storeyed wooden house at the skirts of the Palandöken mountain in Erzurum. Contracted TBC when he was two years old. His father bought a grave for him as the doctors told him he had not more than a few days to live. However, he was cured by concoctions and potions prepared by a peasant woman.

His father, who was in the army, being appointed to a post in Konya, he began his studies in the primary school there. After eight years of study in Konya, the family moved to İzmir. In his first year at the Lycee Namık Kemal, he had a relapse of TBC and had to be hospitalized where he spent three years undergoing a succesful treatment. At the conclusion of which he resumed his studies. During his lycee years he began to work for the Labor Party (TIP) and was elected head of the youth organization of TIP. The last year of his Lycee he abandoned his studies and enlisted in the army. Having completed the basic army training he was sent to Ağrı to serve in the exiles batallion on grounds of his communistic propensities.

Upon the conclusion of his service, he entered the graduation exams and completed his lycee studies successfully. He worked for a fortnight at the Private Organization before resigning his post. He then left for Ankara to pursue his studies. He enrolled in the department of Chinese studies in DTCF (The Languages, History and Geography Faculty of Ankara University.) After a 6 month topography course he began working as topographer in various regions of Turkey as an employee of TEK (Turkish Electricity Organization).

His profession as a poet dates back to his youth in İzmir. He was one of the leading militants during the '68 incidents in Ankara. In the students elections of the DEV-GENÇ (Revolutionary Youth) he was elected member of the federation of students representing the revolutionaries.

His daughter Sanem, from his first wife İpek, was killed in a traffic accident in Turkey. From his second wife Karin he has a son, Kerim, and a grandson Joel.

In the forum organized by the magazine ANT, along with three other young poets, at the end 1969, under the caption of 'The Revolutionay poets declare war', he announced his opinions about the 'New Socialist Poetry', versus the Second New Movement. He affixed his signature on the 'Manifesto of Poems of the '60s'.

In his dissident poems such as *Resist o my Heart/ From our lives/ I am an Asian and my wound is deep/, We will rebuild everything*, etc.. published in such literary magazines as ANT, Halkın Dostları, Türk Solu, Papirüs, Dönem, he became the favorite poet of all the militant students, revolutionary masses and poetry lovers of the time,

His poetry was widely read and recited at student demonstrations and meetings. His first book of poetry published during the said period *We will rebuild everything* was banned. His 'Poems of Protest' carries greater weight at present than at the time it was published.

When the military Junta of 1971 condemned him to 8 year imprisonment (1972) he left the country for Germany where he spent 10 months before going over to Sweden as a political refugee. During 1980-2006 he served as programmer and presenter at Radio Sweden;

and 2006-2008 he worked at the Swedish State Theater as Head of International Theatre and Culture Projects.

As a poet, newspaperman and tourist, he has visited many countries of the world. Actually he is working as a domestic and foreign coordinator and manager or projects related to culture, literature and poetry projects organized in Turkey and abroad. He acts as advisor to cultural organizations in Sweden.

His poems adapted for theatre and his plays are on stages of various nations.

Özkan Mert, considered as the corner stone of modern Turkish poetry, is also known as a Swedish poet.

IMPRESSIONS ON ÖZKAN'S POETRY

We are in the presence of a true poet. His imagery hits the bull's eye.
CEMAL SÜREYYA

You are poetry itself; Poetry which is our only life upon the earth.
İLHAN BERK

Master Özkan is truly grandiose, a poet whose blood circulates in his brain according to his imaginary whims.
SALAH BİRSEL

Is he a magician poet, or a goldsmith this Özkan Mert who sits at poetry's apogee.
MEHMET KEMAL

Come, let me kiss you on your forehead to bless your independent mind challenging the world.
DURSUN AKÇAM

If only we could be a citizen of the world like Özkan Mert.
VEDAT GÜNYOL

I'll have you brought from Stockholm and celebrate your coming in triumphantly with brass band and bugles.
ADALET AĞAOĞLU

Özkan Mert, in the course of his fifty years, had always had his head erect like the head of a racing horse prancing in the world of imagery of poetry.
ADNAN BİNYAZAR

Özkan Mert's poetry as its origin in life itself and encompasses everything in life.
DEMİR ÖZLÜ

Özkan Mert is the second of Homer of Smyrna.
TEKİN ÖZERTEM

You're a creator of splendours.
TALAT S. HALMAN

Özkan Mert's poetry has the taste of an enchanted wine of astutely political taint, smooth and mature, reaching more often than not the perfection of a Brecht or Prévert. No compromise whatever in his verses. The political message is carried in an esthetic garb.
ANA L. VALDES

Özkan Mert's stunning poetry is endowed with the greenery of Lorca's world and Neruda's scintillating sea.
RİKARD HOLM.

Who's on the side of poetry, Özkan Mert say, Governments and armies do not like poetry. Philosophers scared of poetry. Because poetry ear charm, The bead out of philosophy's hands, will steal philosophy's bread. Poetry loves everybody
OKTAY AKBAL

Black Orange

A man bites an orange sideways
The other half missing
In evenings more lost than ever
Getting ready for a raid
With his brown teeth
Having reserved his eyes
For the most beautiful of flowers
Like an unborn child
A negro stops to look at the white
Usurping the sea from the street corner
Scampers tears in his eyes

My Beard As Big As An Apple

I am a modern alchemist.
Here I am with Tuesdays and Fridays!
Unsheathing my alabaster white face from its
scabbard;
my hands are as long as triggers' clicks;
my hands are an eternal musical instrument
in an eternal evening.
It's nearly spring!
Let the day come and the birds sway to and fro, swaying
with everybody else and thinking of something.
Keep a check on our voice.
To its highest pitch have I turned on the volume of my
radio
then turned it off to the lowest. And meditated:
the pageantry of trains and restaurants
passing through the world;
my face dangling in the void.
The smell of raki about my feet,
apple blossoms on trees.
I kept dyeing God;
for I was frantic and hungry;
brimming over my pen-knife in despair
were bird stains.
I'm sort of alcohol color.
I'll tell later about
my defunct acrid days and
the cheekbones of a woman;
for these birds,
this sky, this spring in other words
embitter me.
I mislay
my whistle
on
a

15

tree.
If I don't make love in the park
death is so warm in my mind.

We've controlled our voices
closely observing
a woman, an alcohol.
Full were our beards.
I am recounting a history,
our shapely bodies;
in other words
a corpse
modern, mummified
ceaselessly roaming around;
I am recounting and
recounting.
a city, a forest;
a full blown wind
in my soiled hands
in other words likening
the click of a trigger
to love and autumn
while biting at a sandwich, and crying;
one hand carrying "A VIOLET",
so warm;
everything is so warm and
death
etc.
etc.
etc.
I think.

I'm a savage and dirty virtuoso
cigarette smoke in my mouth;
I am the man waiting for the evening

with a bite of bread that
uses up the day
on the flanks
of a white and infinite instrument.
Not oblivious of the birds
or of everybody else.
I wonder how it would be
going a-hunting in the meadows
merging with streams
taking with me
illustrated publications
doleful stories
love and
de
MOC
racy

I nearly forgot.
I had a beloved once who used to send me
dead butterflies
in envelopes;
you may remember her...

For modern and savage
is my blood;
and my beard is
as big as an apple.
I weep and weep,
I weep as though I was making love to birds,
like the sound of a gun,
a newspaper
in my pocket;
as for photos
later
I throw a flower to the night;

alcohol
wanders in front of my eyes
like a bus.
I am a virtuoso of lust
who clasps and squeezes
women's pudenda,
my hand resting planted there
as though hungry for blood,
awaiting the springtime
looking for the birds and flowers
like a vespertine divinity;
For mummified is the world,
mummified are the spring and the wind
and the trees for that matter;
everything seems so distant now
so far away;

while we
we are
where are we Mr. Christ,
please tell me?

On a Saturday when parks are strewn with embryos
what else can I think about?
with my baritone voice
should I beat time with cymbals
to the night?
Should I bury my heartaches
and my joys at a noontide?
Should I eat opium
and rush
and rush
in my jacket;
why should these instruments

be his instruments
that stroke the body of the autumn;
perhaps I am ready for every contingency,

Ready to listen to Brahms,
to be a snow-white spirit
and fly about in the air;
It's high time that I wept
wept, and wept
What for, though?
If only I found a remedy for living
and found people who killed themselves;
if only the solitude I carry upon my shoulders
turned into a river;

if only I turned birds into cigarettes.
I am a modern alchemist
turning the evening into a carnation;
by the way, what sort of an evening is this evening?
Everything is ready and ready to collapse.
I recover my breath from the mountains
from a provincial evening
I seem to be riding a horse
to be stroking a horse
I loaded my pain and despair
on my day.
I come raising clouds of dust
from calendars that wore out my fingers.
My hands
are birds henceforward;
and my beard is as big as an apple.
Can this be the click of a trigger,
Mr. Christ?

We Will Rebuild Everything

I am in the sky among birds;
on my shirt is a piece of the sun.
I am rolling my shoulders in joy.
A beautiful woman is passing by,
A beautiful tree, a
beautiful child
I am saying: "It is a beautiful thing to live, comrade"
The women-workers are passing by flanking me
Wearing black aprons, with lunch piles in their hands
Not looking at the rising sun, at the sea
At the fruit-sellers and at the fish struggling at the end of
the line
Going to produce tobacco and wine,
Passing by American boats, American flags
and Hatije, fingers bloody from handling the figs, saying
"They have come to buy chewing-gum and women";
And a master bricklayer
spits violently saying:
"It is a damned thing, to live, comrade."
To be dragged around in our land, like a dog,
without being able to resist
with arms tied, humiliated.
The sun grows larger, there are more people;
thousands of people in the streets, at the bus-stops;

Master Halil had been doing the same work for forty
years as a lathe-operator; a veteran of the war for
national independence with three bullet holes in his
chest.

He drives his big car and uses his legs;
He picks up the bourgeois children from their homes,
one by one; boys who have had eggs,
who lack no protein;
boys with silken voices
boys like flowers
good for propagating.
And
He pondered a lot, Master Halil,
on what he would say to his daughter
when she wants an egg;
about his son Mahmut,
who joined a strange political party
which his chief does not approve
while there are other political parties,
who spends his weekly pay
on certain books;
his son whom he wished
he made higher studies.
He dreams of an old dream:
"if I had a workshop of my own...
I should try the sweepstakes again this week... that
sickness of my wife has no end..." ;

thoughts on the most beautiful day;
from time to time especially on Saturdays and Sundays;
he thinks of his friends and often say to them:
"Enver's Winehouse!
You should go there
he has new wines in his cave,
more recordings;
even if he knows something of the other world
he cannot in any way understand

21

this world; how can he,
lathe-operator for forty years
on subsistence wages.

Master Halil
cannot even say:
"It is a damned thing to live, comrade."
He has too much to do
Master Halil.
My mother for years
has been burdened with
the August heat and her cancer.

my mother
hands swollen
from peeling onions

my mother who has not seen
a single beautiful day
these forty years;
shrouds are made
from coarse linen

for our young bodies
magnificent coffins are prepared
from pine, oat and hornbeam wood;
for the little hands, little hearts
for our children who will be born.

To be able to love you,
to be able to love you fully, my country;
to be able to love you fully, my stars, my sky;
to be able to love you fully, my tobacco, my wine, my
everything;

to be able to love you fully my sweetheart;
to be able to embrace you in your dress with floral
designs;
to love you,
to kiss you,
to explain the world to you;
of course,
one day
we will rebuild
everything:
the wine
the tobacco
the stars, the people, and
Turkey

It will be
"a beautiful thing to live"
then;
a beautiful thing to live, comrade.

Hold Out My Heart

Hold out my heart!
Hold out against infamy
and ignominy
Hold out against evil
and the unsightly
against wrong.
Hold out! Don't bite the dust!

How splendid is to live
like a bubbling river,
to ramble through over hill and dale,
with heads touching the clouds
a hot white loaf
under our arm
to go out in the meadows
joining the mass of people
joining millions of men.

That's the way I prefer to tell people
about love and fray
unendingly, without respite.

How do flowers blossom on branches,
how do fish lay eggs
how a baby open its eyes to the world,
that's the way I'd like to live;
how a train glides on rails
how it glides,
that's the way I'd like to live.

I'm brave, o life!
I'm brave, you scoundrels.
With a young heart

do I challenge the world.
O my worn out boots!
I've confidence in you.
Frantic,
I'm marching in streets
with clenched fists;
I sing a song straining my vocal chords;
I live thundering out.

Hold out my heart
Hold out, don't bite the dust!
You are my weapon
my love.
Dead leaves strewn in the streets
dead children
and spring
we carry as shrouds
on our breasts.

Birds flew
over the little houses
whose smells of porridge
pervaded the air;
the street became vermilion
of grief and pain.
To live had become
a dagger
thrust into the flesh
of man.

Hold out my heart!
Hold out, don't bite the dust!
You are my weapon,
my love.

We must hold out baby for a better world:
for the sake of a white loaf of bread
for our innocent loves
we must hold out,
we must!

I'm brave, o life!
I'm brave, you scoundrels.

An immense love has vanished away
turned into a baby grave;
tiny houses with thatched roofs
and the frail bodies
of young people
reminiscent of tender shoots
are bombarded now
all over the world.

My only love is revolution.
You're like water boiling within me;
you're a blossoming new shoot,
my beautiful days not yet lived.

Hold out my heart!
Hold out, don't bite the dust!
You are my weapon,
My love.

My Brave Heart

O glorious trees
my glorious bayonet
my mouth and my fist
my rifle on my shoulder
my canteen
my seminal fluid
and my beloved
beginning thus
to get the picture of a town
of love and death
I must sing a tune
passing by factory chimneys;
my heart
and mottoes and slogans
that unfold me
and everything
and the brown evenings,
the weapons,
the blue devils
and my youth.
O glorious sky, for instance,
how great you are with your inhabitants,
with your brave soldiers.
Twenty thousand years have gone by in flight
from big establishments
from women
with your Toms and Dicks.

For instance,
packs of wolves
and clusters of stars
carry on raids on small hamlets.
Borne are children

who have long forgotten
how to love and
comb their hair,

whose countenances were
imbued with love and
death .
On a train heading for Van
China may well be recounted;
so may also be related
the rosy photograph with floral designs
taken at Khorassan
of a private's wife
in love and tears,
attached to
letters containing dried rose petals.

Thus one must put on,
I reckon the coat nearest to death;
one must tell something to someone,
tell about one's childhood,
how one had kissed Ayşe's belly
her dope addict paramour who
used a razor blade
to defy his enemies;
the breakfast
and the mislaid newspapers;

in the meantime,
loneliness in everybody;
they have learned how to make use
of sadness and pain;

out came books on Marx and love

meant for
water melon sellers, generals and infatuated love;
the sky and the drink
laid out;
and they spoke and spoke
spoke and they spoke;
there were mustachioed men with pallid countenances
with bellies saturated with alcohol
and loneliness;
who opened their eyes to life
with onions and raki.
A white song
nestled in my heart,
in my glorious heart;
on the one hand, pigeons
spring odors
joy of life
with hands and feet tied;
on the other,
I am befuddled
shouting
calling out
to restaurants
to waiters
to mountains and towns,
shouting
shouting
the echoes of those
ice cold girls
reverberating
through my heart.
I take a sip
from my drink
and light a cigarette.

It's the month of July,
Darling, I say, darling of mine,
my hands outgrow
the Earth.
Taxis and birds pass by,
the smell of porridge and
the spring odors
pervade my room.
Okras strung on a string;
a bedstead for two;
supposing I get married, I say to myself
I might give up drinking then
and the acacias, and
my vagrancy.
But the rebel within me
the anger that
feeds me grows out of proportion
I rush out of my room
heading for asphalted streets,
to the parks and everywhere
I run
and run,
getting lost among slogans and placards,
and march
along with mustachioed
men with pallid countenances
and march with women.
whose lips are red with blood
instead of with lipstick

I march
and march
and march…

AND I PROTEST THE WORLD.

What Will I Call Life

Oh, grey, hazy sky
My love is growing with you
Something that I call life
is sticking in my throat.

I can already sharpen
a knife on my wrists;
I can expose my chest to the world;
the squares are teeming
with thousands of people
and me by your side;
O, grey, hazy sky!
We can tell the children
whose faces are crystal pure as a blue mountain spring
about happiness we never experienced.

This is why our fists are growing,
our hearts are growing.
There is no doubt;
probably I'm in love,
perspiring with excitement
as I look at the world.
My hands are reaching everywhere
as a machine gun.

But still I'm afraid
to pick a flower
to love a woman
as though I could exhaust
all the loves
of the world.

O, grey, hazy sky !

I am stretching my hands toward you,
the blood in my veins
is splashing over treachery and dishonesty.
In my heart are love and belief,
by my side is the grey, hazy sky.

I will not die
even if I'm embroidered by bullets like a canvas.

A legacy from my grandfather
is to roar like thunder while dying.

I've inherited it from my grandfather
Who used his scimitar with the skill of a jewellery cutter
to stand erect like a mountain upon the earth.

Love and belief
must stand out like a fortress

and the happiness
must be stamped like a seal
on treachery and dishonesty
so must one read this poem.

1969 / Ankara

Dear Boy

It arrives in a city aboard a train;
carried are
the blossoming meadows
bereft of their poppies
in the small train stations
of small towns;
what is experienced is a
very thin line. Spleen.

Your hair
I used to comb with my fingers
long long ago…

I'm staring at the city's architecture
regardless of the angle through which I'm observing
the sky seems always visible
so are
the towers of this city
built by thousands of boys;
and its meadows.

It seems to me
that we keep on forgetting
certain things.
All those loves eventually
came to naught.
Those men
went away,
in their pockets
the photographs
of the split of time.

No one could get hold
of each other's sorrow.

In my countenance appears now
an unpardonable youth,
fresh blood
straw flame
pigeon flying
over my wounds.
The plum trees I grazed,
large roses,
the first city I led into temptation.
O dear boy!

Warmth around my shoulders
day lost
day recovered
a dirty yellow.
Woman
is luminous;
her lips are
cherry stones.
I dote
on parrot blue trains
carriages loaded with fancies.

Five minutes before departure
all the cities I have been to;
your belly taut and functional
the heat
that runs down my spine.

The heart I carry
like a pamphlet
has remained intact
for twenty thousand years.
Come on, tell me something

warm me up
dear boy.

Can it be
that grapes
are already mellow?

Welcome Welcome

Welcome! Welcome
friends to this new country.
Sicilian peasants,
Spaniards with full beards,
Turks with gold crowned teeth…
Princes of a beastly sorrow
and heroes of a modern fairy tale.

You are coming
through a sad and interminable song.
Your news is all over the dailies,
all over the wavelengths, and heard by
the outpost sentinels of Europe.
The wheels of the black train you boarded
are not of iron, but of Turkish delight.

Welcome! Welcome
to this new country, my friends.
You are fleeing from steppes and hunger,
from jails and armies
-to spare the children and the peoples-
the cold Swedish sun
cannot warm your hearts.
You will unload from ships
meat, cement, bananas and water melons.
You will cover the roads with bitumen.
O the greasy vapor, emitted
by huge washing machines
filling your lungs. It will make you feel
as though you had swallowed a frog.

One gets used to everything.
It won't take you more than a week

before you fail to perceive a smell or a sound.
You know well enough that
we are not invited to this country
for the sake of our curly hairs and dark eyes.
Let alone that the sky here is hardly ever blue.

Welcome! Welcome
to this country, my friends!
No more alas the pillow on which you put your head,
no more the matinal cock crow
that shreds the sky to pieces,
no more the wooing of the ring doves.

Here you'll abide for years
imagining to return home
all day long every day.
No Penelope no king of Ithaca
will be waiting for your return home.
You're but a pontoon bridge
stretched between the past and the future.
Aha! April is in;
nature's putting on all its finery.

The snow of the mountains transformed into water
in gaiety flows into the earth's womb.
Birds, the rivers' progeny
return to their nests
with fishes in their beaks.
Now, insert a cassette into the cassette-player,
I want to hear a tune, a lively air
from the black plains of the Aegean region;
many years have gone by
since we last heard the sound of drum.
What do you say to a chicken roasted in the oven now,
served with French fries...

How else can one endure this life, my friend!

Fröken! A cup of white coffee please!

2.

The sun over the Baltic Sea,
a fish quivering at the extremity of the line.
Gypsies began coming downtown from the heights;
carrying a fiddle in one hand and
a bottle in the other.
Come on, write a letter home
tell about the snow that fell this winter
and the flakes,
toys for our children.

The gray sky of Stockholm
speckled with bluish patches,
a couple of dipsomaniacs asleep
leaning against each other on a bench .
Bruises on their mouth;
must be a consequence of a fall from the staircase.

Emigrés pass by,
one of the dipsomaniacs wakes up and
rushes at them to ask for a crown.
Having failed to get what he asks,
goes back to resume his sleep where he'd left it.
Among the émigrés, the shortest of them all,
is busy undoing the buttons of her wife in her
imagination.

3.

Flower girls at the farmers' market. An old hag
declares that the end of the world is nigh. A cross in her
hand,
she chants.
A girl with skirts rolled up her waist
with snow-white legs
stretched on stone steps
is imbibing the sun with open palms

Swedish policemen in trench coats wearing white gloves
are making their rounds.
An ignorant person
would likely take them for princes
defected from a Lilliputian country;
they dally with walkie-talkies like children
as though they were toys.
Among the émigrés
the one rather shortest of them
has ended unbuttoning her wife's robe;
now astride on her,
begins squeezing her full breasts.
Darkness surges before his eyes:
his countenance brightens,
his bones warm up...
makes for the bench occupied by the dipsomaniacs
and give them a ten crown piece
as though he were leaving a brothel.

4.

The sun is like a boy squinting,
peeping through a half-open curtain
of gray clouds.
O what a lovely autumn day!
It strips the Earth stark naked.
Golden leaves, leaves of silver,
flying about in the air
like herds;
the autumn is the golden crown
of the Baltic Mother.
Oh how charming they look
the policewomen of Stockholm;
marching with manly steps,
trying to disguise their natural feminine charm,
they amble beating the air
as though pounding
with the bottom of their white belly
the man supine on the bed.
With their guns dangling on their curvy hips;
pull on their white gloves
on their slim fingers, and
move away toward the sea.
An émigré with a handlebar mustache,
may be a Turk or a Spaniard,
vehemently twists his mustache.
An American tourist accosts one of them;
would you please stand
beside me for a photo?
His chubby better-half
fumbles for the right button to press;
a little to the left please, she says,
let me have fount

now, say cheese please!
Tick tock, there you are!
Thank you very much
Very, very much indeed!
Come now dear, time for some fish and chips
before we proceed on to the Modern Museum;
Picasso is waiting for us, you know.

In the middle of the park called 'The King's Garden',
a vast space where a game of chess is on the go,
one of the players is a puny émigré.
He looks as though someone had dwindled him,
by squeezing him in his palm.

He has difficulty in moving the pieces,
almost as tall as himself
from one of the checker to the next;
the other player is a seven feet high
Swedish.
Looks as though someone had stretched him like a
rubber band.
It's been more than an hour now that
he has been thinking about which piece to move.
The passive spectators grown tired of watching them
have opened their newspapers to browse the news.

A young girl is bending toward the pond to get
some water; with the water in her palm
she wets her breasts basked in the sun.

Life Death And History

Having stopped at small stations
where oranges are sold we arrived..
There my country! My friends and
my slim-waisted tea glass;
our young world smells of flowers and corpses
no matter where you are.

O so big is the sun! As big as a broad-brimmed hat,
and as warm as a human face;
thawing snow waters herald the spring.

The dawn encompasses the city like a red forest,
a child with wiry eyes in love
getting prepared to take a rest
in the bosom of a balmy evening.

The blue trains exchange kisses
like butterflies made of iron
on the bridges.

History repeats itself in disguise.
A newborn
with blood stains on it still fresh.

A child grows up swaddled
by a thousand year old affliction.
Who can ever seal your breast my child?
Who can ever divide the running waters with a blade?

I, who am coming through the streets where stars are
dancing,
listening to a tango within me smuggled from the
Aegean Sea

and the vestiges of balmy August evenings
of a blue love.

You may stretch with pleasure now, o the Mediterranean
Sea!
A boy may hold you by the hand to take you to his
mother
riding a bicycle made of gently blowing wind.

Who has planted these towns here?
Who shaped the clay of life?
The young children of history, surely.

The hands that never grow old
sew the best attires for history;
heartaches had been their favorite toys...

Life, death and history!

Come on, take off your clothes, fling them away to the
dawning sun.
Let your words pass through a blue love.
Keep in your mind those who kissed life in midmorning
for the last time.

It's as though an enormous grief is riding in a carriage in
the sky.

My Name Is Peace

My name is Peace
I'm coming from Asia,
Africa and Europe,
Australia and America...

My name is Peace
I'm coming from thousand years war,
From tears of mothers deprived of their sons,
From the children that atom bomb
turned into ashes.

My name is Peace.
I'm coming from the outer space.

My name is Peace. I've come
to transform the world into
"An ocean of peoples and friendship

1984 / Stockholm

Swedish Beauties

Swedish beauties pass by me
Beauties that beggar description
On their lapels Vietnam badges
Beauties indoctrinated
With the idea of freedom
Wearing blue jeans
They live in the course of one day
What our girls experience in ten years

To describe them what love is
and what freedom is
is like describing a bus to someone
who never saw a bus in his life.

Lund University

A white stone building
in a park
in a Bergman film
I had imagined
a human being distributing diplomas,
whereas I was
and have ever been
someone with
hands, feet
and
a heart.

The Dome

I'm passing by the Dome
I believe that this tower
always illuminated-at night-is haunted.
I think that one or two of its priests must suicide
And whenever I pass by the Dome
I am looking for
Corpses of priests
at the foot of towers.

My Heart A Violent In The Middle of Earth

Locked in an embrace the world and I
in a vast space swarming with stars and lights
my heart is a violet in the middle of the Earth.

A streaming tango on my lips,
am I hunting life or is life hunting me
under an orange sky?

In the coffee-houses of a Scandinavian city
beleaguered by orange hours
you're but a passive spectator
even of your very heart.

Low spirits in these northern cities
taste of spirits,
and whenever I kiss a Finnish beauty on the throat
a mark is left wild red on her lips.

O the exiles, sons and daughters of weird dreams!
The blue negresses of blue evenings!
Tell me the destination of those vessels carrying your
heart!
Who will hand out bouquets to you under the snow?

My heart is a pigeon nest
cast over by a pale cloud of smoke.
Am I letting loose pigeons to ride the skies, or my grief?
Who's that singing on the cross, can it be me?

I am planting a big kiss on your cheeks
our beloved Earth
a lukewarm wine is our life even today;

Stockholm smells of the Mediterranean whenever it rains.

The Pigeons Are Shaking The World

On the shoreline of your face
I'm confronting a wet autumn;
the shadow of the mountains on your bosom falls,
provincial maidens with crimson cheeks sealed,
timid and deferential,
wriggle when they catch sight of me.

THE PIGEONS ARE SHAKING THEIR BREASTS

A crowd marches toward us with backs stabbed;
the armies of grief raise their hands
renting the sky grudgingly. Commotion!
The history is in confusion.

THE PIGEONS ARE SHAKING THE HISTORY.

As I flee a city
another city surges before me.
My eyes are sore from watching the world
Watermelon sellers are eating meat balls
under the street lamps;
Children who forgot how to spin a top
in the shadow of the twilight
reminiscent of stacked rifles
are at attention;
my people
stand to attention

THE PIGEONS ARE SHAKING THE CITY

My mouth is glued to the mountains.
A blue vest thrown over my shoulders
my business is to bombard life

with words
I have burnt my address book
and the howling of jackals.

THE PIGEONS ARE SHAKING ME.

The Sun Was My Kite

To be imbued with poetry is to be permeated with love,
and a speeding train is seduction
while the sky is
its despondent umbrella.
No, we're not watching a film;
nor are we coherent sentences of a book.
Our dreams are not factory made.

We're climbing a ladder put up against the sky
If you've already had your breakfast, come with me!
Let's exchange kisses with clouds.
Mr. Christ, you!
You'd better stay where you are;
Yes, you!

Who is not fascinated by a red poppy field!
I wish I had a shirt
poppy color
and the sun my kite.
Who could hold me back?
"To hell with the world," I said,
"the sun was my kite."
"You don't say!"

You know it, of course. The sun cannot possibly be a kite.
"Do fish not make love under the water?"
asked my son to me.
"They sure do, Kerim," I said.
"They get boozy even when they kiss."
"And their tails?"
"They simply redden."

This is a poetry:

you may either believe in poetry or in fish, as you like.
or in Kerim or even me for that matter.
What does the Koran say by the way?
"Believe not in poets!" does it not?

A Swarm of Birds Is My Beard

We are all children of those blues.
Somewhat rural, yet bearing city scars,
wearing shirts, a fantastic witch's brew,
for the love arrested in a June evening.

-Ours beards are like flocks of birds

"Watchmen of spleen' they called us,
grown up among starlings and oak groves;
infatuated with the Earth and
touching the chord of a violin.

-Ours beards are like flocks of birds

Hot jazz resounded on the radio
rain showered on me like a nerve-racking book
for the provincial girls with ruddy cheeks
I began crying in the early hours of the morning

-A swarm of birds is my beard.

It's true I did make love in God's acres
during summer nights when I stole apricots and flowers
and had an affair with a mysterious blonde maiden,
and great has been the number of my evil deeds.

-A swarm of birds is my beard.

We are all children of those blues.
A tipsy pigeon has brought us up
rain drew our portraits
on balconies warmed by the sun.

-Our beards are like flocks of birds.

I am collecting motley pebbles on the shore.
I extracted a handful of sky
from inside a black mussel
The fish are as drunk as I am, but...

-A swarm of birds is my beard.

My heart is as inflated today
as the accordion of a gypsy.
Starlings and humans swarm the city,
taverns are thronged with thousands of Robinsons

-A swarm of birds is my beard.

A narrow path in a wood
is a man's life lost to view in a green forest
even though entangled with
oleander trees, lakes and cocoons.

-A swarm of birds is my beard.

We are all children of those blues.

-Our beards are as blue as the birds.

Tender Is My Life

In buckets did they steal
the moonlight from the sky
where birds hung like censers.

Jazz songs flashed
on the radio;
a black woman
with a sulfurous voice
in whom sorrow's hat
moaned in melodies.

I, in a street
just opened for pedestrians,
combed by face
with the fresh blue of
the Mediterranean.

My face is mine already
oven where fiery morns are kindled.

All doves are young at noon
All rains red
Without my knowledge
I saw my heart turned into Robinson.

Rome is an open country
like your lips dearest
the lioness that bit the wind
has brought be up
through the concealed
skirts of mountains
I was incensed by her breasts.
This is why my life is tender and erotic
My life a revolution.

57

It was a gypsy beauty that stole my virility
In a blue prairie.
A sea aflame went by
then the blue accordion sounds.
My life is spent in the company of
Winds, women and revolutions
in fighting and kissing each other.

Keep Your Dreams Deep Blue, Your Heart Hot Red

Tomorrow is another day…
Everything will be more beautiful and
The sun will dazzle your eyes more tomorrow
And a warm pair of palms will cover yours…
A hat of blue clouds will be on your head
And you will say nice and sweet things
To your lover with flower full of eyes

Tomorrow is another day…
And everything more beautiful
You may not have a job, you may not have any money
And you may be craving for a hot slice of bread
Your lover with flower full of eyes may leave you…
this is life, you never know…
but never lose hope
believe me tomorrow will be another day

Tomorrow is another day
And everything more beautiful
Nothings ands
Roses will suddenly bloom at the point where
Your eyes fail to see anything ahead
Keep your dreams blue
And your heart hot red
Tomorrow is another day
And we are the owners of tomorrow

İf tired: go rest
İf thirsty: have a sip of water
İf lonely: go have a couple drinks with a friend
Or go make love all night long
But do come back later

Tomorrow is another day
Tomorrow we will paint the world with roses

A Dark Blue Tango In The Baltic Sea

I had once a modern voice
I'd shoot with my rifle over over again
As the jet planes rent asunder the sky
A blue Stockholm

Would you believe
Even after a dark green tropical drink
I used to pilfer myself
Shouldering the torn doves of the night

O what pilfering!
inserting and pressing a rose on my heart
I fought the carriages of sorrow
Like a raped symphony

It is true that I was an albatross
that kindled its eyes while flying
to thrust its shaggy beard into women's mouths
that I sang songs forgotten

I exchange kisses at night with reindeers under the night
sun
As the snowflakes hit me like dust of jewels
A warm Mediterranean blue sways before my eyes
The world rolls on like a glass bead
The rifles I shot with is discussed at households
In the virgin lakes of the North
The sorrows I shot at and the blondes I pilfered
My heart is a passage opening to the world

Letting doves kiss my rent heart
I dance with a dark blue tango in the Baltic Sea.

Turmoil's Of May

Who assembled us in this world?
It's a question
reminiscent of a clash with a violet.

O the meadows!
A wrong answer to my youth
I know you by heart.

Everybody can pile up a city
in front of one's heart. The first streets
where we had exchanged kisses
turned now into a stream.

Regardless of the paths your heartaches may have taken
The drink we drink is cloud color, raki color in other
words, and
our domicile is the World.

Your breasts have grazed me,
then your perfumes. Fascination!
You have turned our love into a republic.

All right! Let's carry on to tomorrow
whatever we can. I'd like to attach a stream on your hair?
crush me now with your red lips reminiscent of grapes.

If a slender spleen has portrayed your heart
acacias besieged it
What's wrong with this love?

O summer follies, southerly winds
O my bleeding youth… a negative film is my life
under a nocturnal sun.

Make a call to your heart. Ask the birds!
The cluster of stars brimming over my beard stained
with blood
is a piece of sensational news for the television screen.

It was a chemical explosion
my first encounter with,
carnations
and girls.

A city in summer disarray
in mid winter: Bodrum
The streets are swept by winds
wherein Kurdish workers mosey along.

Sunday: the boat to Karşıyaka
packed with cadets
the inside of their caps bearing Atatürk's snapshot.

It can no longer be concealed from people
the fact that I arrived in the world
riding a rose leaf.

How lucky I am! I was even able
to comb my hair.
I had the privilege of exchanging kisses with a river.

My birth was a philandering
affair: October
geography: the Palandöken mountain range.

It is reported that when I first butted
against my mother's breasts
I happened to be a tiny drunkard

in close embrace with the entire world

You who carry about you a street with eyes grayish blue,
that street is the audible history of love;
your mouth smells of apples glued to mine.

Indeed, we can all commit murder
picking up flowers or lapsing into silence.
God with rosy countenance chides us.

I am working on poetry and storms
I'm kindling my words brushing them
against a maiden's cheeks never been kissed before.

Poetry is time's flames
and the multitude of loneliness
It scolds not only the living, but also the dead.

I'm taking off my shirt in the midst of May disarray
and hanging it on a willow branch. A river
passes through it. I'm directing a street

bigger than a streetcar toward the sky;
oranges that kindle the Mediterranean coast
scorch me; and your eyelashes.

The May disarray, the southerly winds,
scorching are the waters of thawing snows.
May, like a butter-fly, flies about on the shore of my face.

What's happening to us?
Turn off this tango,
it smashes the flower beds.

Attention This Poem Is Meant To Tease The World

Yes, I call the Adriatic Sea to witness!
I'm teasing the restaurants.
I'm teasing the republics.
How can we otherwise cover up
our defection to the world?
The world is the place of encounter of us all
Somebody else may differ, but
for me, the most interesting, the most thrilling thing in
life
are women and
rivers,
and last but not least poetry…

This city I've passed through a fair handsome morning
riddling it with my terrorist verses
turns into the smallest republic of
love and anger
when you kiss me;
but my exchange of kisses with a city
with a woman,
with myself
is meant to make the languorous butter-flies
of my childhood fly
to the present time?

In order to compose myself
I'm teasing
love and the world.
My only witnesses are
words, simply words
and the meridians.

I'm asking now:

whose evening
have we stolen?
Why should each of us not have
an admirable
evening?

Everything may be put to sale perhaps: love,
Submarines, news agencies
rockets with nuclear heads
revolutions
world tours, battles, hunger and child mortality,
banana republics,
train stations and winds…

The Silence

In between,
the explosions
of two bombs,
governs
our world.

Peron's body was stolen from his grave
with his hands cut off.
The tango, the football and
the Falkland defeat
30.000 murders;
Buenos Aires, the heart of Argentine,
a city that could have been still
bigger and handsomer;
Turkey's anger vie with the Argentine's.
The Israeli soldiers break
the arms and shoulders
of Palestinian young men
using rocks and boulders.

I want to purify the world of its stains by
striking it against the mountains.

O God! How furious I am!

God And Tango

I'm a luminous exile;
my house is the bull's-eye of the world.

Ruffle my hair! Prepare me for love
make a river pass through my teeth.

Swap all the epaulettes
for white doves.

Like splinters of mirrors
we'll multiply by a series of mutual reflections.

I made this wine from the grapes
that had first seen the sun upon the earth.

I am bathing my words in this wine,
history is in hot pursuit of me.

If history and rivers disentangle me,
here I am! Here are God and the tango!

I'll be the first émigré,
to grow lettuce on the moon.

I'll be sending the odor of pine to the world,
if not by letter, then by stars.

EVERY EXILE IS BUT A BROKEN TRIANGLE AND
FREEDOM THE LAST DROP OF BRANDY
MOUTHWASH.

I am a luminous exile,
Solitude is my headmaster.

They hung my heart
between Turkey and the world

Who can warm up my youth's cold valleys
trampled by military trucks rumbled past?

A yellow land is ablaze within me;
I dodge my flushing face from people.

Astor Piazzola raises the sea
with a single tango.

Astor and I we are laying siege on time.
Who has ironed our shirts with sadness, we know not.

Poetry is a pirate may be,
a time thief with a ruddy beard.

Your hips a canary darling,
a den of terror.

Canaries sprout
wherever I kiss

A saxophone climbing to silence hunts us,
and meteorites shoot among us.

I AM A LUMINOUS EXILE, A BROKEN TRIANGLE
FREEDOM THE LAST DROP OF BRANDY
MOUTHWASH

Don't Cry For Me O Turkey OF Mine

Don't cry for me o my Turkey
Don't cry o stars and sky of mine
Don't my cold nights, deserted streets
I will be back
From faraway lands and seas
Even though my heart
is tossed around like a shipwreck.

Don't cry o big country
Don't my sad and distressed country!
We
Your sons and daughters
Flowers of exiles and prisons
We'll come back to your with tepid rains
As though returning to mother's womb

We'll bring you all the suns we've gathered
and affections. For we died
for the sake of a sunny country
we died for affections
And freedom.

Don't cry o my big country
My sad and distressed country
Don't please!
Let others cry but not you

If they ask our name
Just say it was a single word

Freedom!
Freedom!
Freedom!

Love Is The Venice Of Us All

Poetry is the empire
of betrothed maidens and marquis.
I, who was brought up courting music;
look, I am posing for a river.
This is the reason why cities dreams of me;
this is the reason why I came
after having scythed a street.
The occupation of a room we had taken up
was a sign denoting the impossibility of catching
the ray of light in my exiled heart

-Love is the Venice of us all.

Poetry is more accessible to me
than a sparrow.
Every spot where my mouth begins with the morning
is a den of terrorism of course.
Neither paved roads nor fleets can save me,
a barbarian with a scathing look.
For my heart has been prohibited like a jazz musician
from Prague.
Yet it is a land covered with heath, Chagal it is…
the best answer being the irreversibility of sorrow.

-Chagal is the elder brother of us all.

Revolutions, eroticism, plants, birds' leftovers
and heath reveal us: a bleeding history
is our defense.
When I turn you round to face me clasping you by your
hips
is a festivity challenging death.

71

A poppy in your hand leaning on the sky
you swiftly pass by through a narrow and yellow street;
a narrow street is everybody's knowledge;
the blue child cannot possibly evade their faces,
run away no matter how hard he tries.

-Children's faces have no telephone number.

No, nothing
will ever go by without being hit by my words.
Even though my heart is shattered like a barren land
I shall bear witness to you all! To our age!
In some corner of the Earth
my breast is thronged with cranes and
I am dancing to the tune of blustery winds.
Young and tender a morning is my weapon,
whose butt is engraved
with marks of my younger years and of sadness.

-You know, don't you, İzmir is my diary.

Jazz And Carnations

Humans, carnations, jazz
and the world
reach me having stabbed my portrait.
Whatever was stolen in the small hours of the morning
I am stealing the same
from the Earth.
Trains pass through my room,
restaurants
Winds
Hissing bullets
and child faces rent asunder
in the uterus
over a blue river.

Were I to depict a river
-but a blue one-
I'd have depicted I think
all the children
that died of starvation, in wars.

-Who's then the worst bloody tyrant in history?

All right, you did well
In letting me stretch your belly a little too taut
so that moonlight spurted from my gun;
ours are now all the children of the fall.
Whoever entangled
violets in my beard

whoever is wherever
Wherever I've pegged my jacket
Wherever the world has been swirled
I am there swaying in the air

with a scorching heartache
reminiscent
of a
Moaning
Saxophone.
If we consider our world as
a collection
on which are pasted
dried corpses of soldiers
And the burnt bodies of
young men whose hearts had been ripped
out from their bodies
Under torture
there our era is reigning!
there each of us is called 'Freedom'
That history will record.

My poetry plunders the world
what I insinuate by words is
the orgasm of rivers and doves.
I kidnap myself
Through balconies
That move me away from the Earth.

The plaster of my heart
was applied
with the raped
April evenings.
Although my chest
has been rent asunder
by dense marquis
what I offer you
Every morning
is flowery rivers.

An argentine tango on the radio,
you know,
is more proletarian
than its American brother
jazz music.
Born in the brothels of Buenos Aires,
Its father Astor Piazella
Is still reigning
As a dirty yellow light thief
In all the Argentinean loves and us.
While I and Astor whose hearts are
Somewhat more daring
Are asking now:

-Who traced the portrait of the sea on our lips?

I've taken up my pen in 1988
as though beginning a poem
dangerous and fugitive. I thought
what would poetry mean
for Huseyin, the grocer?
The juvenile wind and heavy heart
a sweet lie, perhaps.
I wonder where exactly a kilogram of white cheese
might be stored in the heavenly vault?
The feeling might be incomprehensible, but
I fear that barking of dogs may sound no more
in 'the Star Wars'.
Who would tell about the small town
Asleep in the lap of acacias?
To whom can we describe the bliss one experiences
while holding in one's hands
the tiny feet of a newborn.
Well then, it's plain

-Peace is life's fiancé.

Silence everybody! I'm going to sing
to the mountains, rocks, trees and rivers
I intend to animate the world
just like Australian aborigines
by singing songs.
Silence! If we keep silent,
we might perhaps hear
the dialogues between
the fishermen of Istanbul
and the Chinese philosophers.
We can prick our ears to Prague's heart
from Bebek
in a misty November afternoon.

Silence! If we keep silent,
We may perhaps see
the rosy breasts of the fiancé bitten by
an infantry soldier from Khorassan while on leave.
Silence!
A generation annihilated by bullets and in gallows
Is parading before you
S i l e n c e!
A whole generation of victims
parading before you killed with bullets
S i l e n c e!
He was thrown in front of history
as a piece of bloody flesh
We are lying now in a coffin
to the accompaniment of chants,
expectations
and colorful dreams.
But
Consider my friend

-whose coffin has history been?

Poetry Does Not Drink Coffee

Poetry does not drink coffee, it commits murder
and plays at billiards with empires.
He passes his hat through the Suez Canal
hitting abysmal heights.

I've already told you:
what made me rebellious was life and books.
My temple is a world
woven with bullet burns and violets.

Wherever I turn my gaze I see an invisible window
in it an immense heaven.

A bitter youth in frenzy
means letting moonlight pass
through a bombarded rice field
and nicknaming all the rivers.

I'm fishing out an octopus
from beneath the skyscrapers;
an old creature five million years old
in the depths of aquatic chambers

I'm drinking beer in Hamburg
with hunters of eels and cacao traders.
Elbe runs at its leisure; not in a hurry, it seems.
Left Prague for quite some time now.

Erotica the greatest solitude à deux,
the naked summary of our self-revelation..

Poetry does not drink coffee, it commits murders
It knows the weakest point of its addressee;

its weapon is but an image as sharp as a razor blade;
it first embraces its victim with affection,
then begins shedding tears.

Dream And Reality

Can history
Be a dream
In which
Horses
Kings
and dead peoples
Flourish.

Decapitated heads of kings
were thrown now and then
before peoples
-like in 1789-
not to let them be understood
that it was them that had
'transfused blood'
into history.

My Headgear Is Lake Van And Not A Hat

I've got a harmonica
Where birds drink water
I'm hiding
the city's parks in it.

Parks that are the domicile of a people
And the first stop of love
It's there that is recorded
the story of the first kiss.

Whenever I kissed a girl
In a park
My headgear was Lake Van and not a hat.

A Moon In Bodrum In Lemon Colour

Mr. Bougainvillea, yes you!
So handsome
in Bodrum,
yet…

How pleasantly you lean over to the world,
From Tülin's terrace,
In your purple/ violet
undershirt.

All the seductive girls
wear tonight
not earrings
but a moon in lemon color.

Everybody's is a river
in Bodrum
hanging on his bedpost
after lovemaking.

Mediterranean Landscapes

Antalya: a city kidnapped
from the Aegean
To be betrothed to the Mediterranean.

In its coral gown
it lets southerly winds
suckle at its breasts.

Further down the island restaurants
a handful Mediterranean.

I'm swimming beneath the rocks.
Arabesque melodies pollute
me and the Mediterranean.

On the balcony shared by Metin and Günsel
breakfast is a revolution.
As the mountains across
graze past your hair,
the Mediterranean
gets mixed in your tea.

Peasant girls
with rounded hips and
breasts never been kissed before
stroll through the streets
of Antalya
in a glorious erotic air,

a boiled cob in hand.

Balıkova is an Aegean village.
During the hail storm in May

83

it had entered the poem uninvited
in the raki we drink.

Can it be Ziya that had the shad
drink raki at our table;
as it began to sing a song.

A gentle melody is a sea of sorrow
and touches the heart as a sharp blade.
It's handsome
and endless and white like a pigeon.

How puzzled you look!
Had it not been for Nihat and the lilies
in this poem.

There! Hail has evolved into rain
absorbing the salt of the white cheese
in the wet plate.

This poem has got wet;
If you don't want to get wet
dear reader,
better not read it!

Istanbul redolent with the scent of lily
is my fiancé.
We live apart in separate quarters
except in June and July.
It occupies a place
In each of my poems

Incontestably!

Is this the end of the poem?

Let those who say YES
lower their hands.

Mozart And The Mediterranean

The image of Mozart and the Mediterranean in my
pocket,
I am on my way on a violet exile
to become a tenant of mountains and rains.

I am measuring my life in terms of pains, deaths and
oceans.
I've left endless days behind me full of affection that had
revealed me;
Now, with glorious eroticism, I'm washing my wounds
in the Atlantic Ocean.

I'm kissing your nipples exposed to the wind
I'm kissing your mouth the most sensual in the world.
For, I am a slave to love and to the scent of rose.

I am as though seated within a double-bass,
my body rent asunder in the poppy fields;
in all my photos rains and sorrow shower.

Mine is a sorrow carried by a yellow street-car;
its wick has the taste of the Amasya apples.
That must be the reason: a sad tune is
my face;
the cigarette between my lips is thinner than the wing of
a butterfly.

How you debilitated the splendid young men in prison
cells;
we died, we were exiled, but we never surrendered.

A new age is dawning from the spikes of suffering.
Come on! Geometry notebooks and color pencils!
We'll trace a brand new sky.

86

Can you feel the stars breathe?
You also have a star and a little sky…
squeezed in between two streets.

A full moon color red wine
swaying to and fro between
the collars of your white shirt.
Hold it! Let your hands turn into pigeons.

The image of Mozart and the Mediterranean in my
pocket,
wherever I go I am an exile;
rain and sorrow shower on in all my photographs.

And the exiles have no God.

Who's On The Side Of Poetry

Governments and armies
Do not like poetry

Holy books, prophets
and laws
are dead against poetry

Philosophers scared of poetry
Because poetry ear charm
The bead out of philosophy's hands
will steal philosophy's bread

Virgin nuns
secretly fondle poetry

But poetry does not care:
it owes nothing to nobody.
It leaves a storm
At the door of history
and pose its own way

Poetry loves everybody

Translated from the Turkish
By Feyyaz Kayacan

Good-Bye Sweetie
Good-Bye Cadillac

My chest in disarray
I roam the cold cities of Europe;
Turning over my thin and bitter mustache
On parks and canals.

In the most naked hours of the night,
when prostitutes of Stockholm mosey along the streets
I'm suddenly caught by a poem:
by a poem in search for its address and jacket.

With scorching words in my mouth
I stretch myself out and kiss
the innermost recesses of life and the poem
brave to the bitter end and beautiful.

My deserted and rebel heart!
that nobody can reach,
you are a convict
squeezed between the meridians!

We are the only vestiges of canaries and streets burdened
with acacias
in the shade of loves and arms
children whose eyes are big as big can be
and sorrowful as sorrowful can be.

It may be because of this, the words we use are stainless,
Bedeviled and rebellious;
that's why we are armed;
our weapon is the melancholy of a small village

I once had a mouth organ
almost a blue '57 Cadillac;

I took around on a red streetcar
the tunes I composed at dawn.

Your lips I know by heart as fresh as ever
a preface to our love
a rebellious spring and İzmir.

Good-bye darling! Good-bye Cadillac, dearie!

Can you hear me, my blue Cadillac?
The poem within me grows like a murder;
an April morning aroused and naked
Raped by rain drops..

Bodrum (Halikarnasos)

Bodrum's white stone houses
Doves of my heart
Their bluishness turned round the corner
Their white chimneys have turned into sails

I turned into a cloud and settled on the sofa
Seagulls made their nests in my hair
I drank too much and turned into a beauty
Staring at the mountains I turned into a bird.

Your eyes have turned into violets,
Waist in perspiration
I strewed Turkish delight in your skirt
So that I might bite your lips.

Where Are Your Stars Amsterdam?

How does one embark on a man, on a city,
on a grim Monday about to come off from calendars
with violet carnations – planted in petroleum tins -
in terraces, on stone steps…

A green stream runs through the night;
wounded are the acidified towers and the weary parks of
the city;
no matter what the hour is
the sky is not utterly devoid of hope.

Let's talk if you like with words as light as a dove
wishing each other happy hours ruthlessly.
But then let everybody reveal his identity and merits.
For our aim is to cleanse life.

What 'I'm going to tell concerns you all;
you are all bound to listen to what I'm going to say;
let me be a glowing piece of cloud and you stars
illuminating the Earth and washing the winds.

My life rushes toward the sun at breakneck speed.
I am passing by the most famous cathedral of Europe
Wall writings, wall paintings, the stark naked poems of
life,
the stark naked faces in a stark naked city.

A single glance from you will suffice to identify them;
like trees uprooted and toppled over
like ashes falling from a cigarette, they are;
with eyes as sharp as a blade.

Our life is as taut as the skin of a drum.

Your heart may be as cold as a jewel under the snow.
You are condemned to winds and sorrows;
but you know there is no path to take without affliction
and affection.

Regardless of the hour, there is always hope

Beware! Today may be the inception of a doomed love
affair
even though it may be a sad one, even though the hope
concealed in the dark
Have faith in me. It's settled, we'll be washing life.

I'm walking along a canal in Amsterdam,
a dark blue tango on my lips.
Is the evening setting in? Or am I floating in a sea of
dejection?
Lukewarm is the night; and I think
my heart is bleeding.

Houses are stuffed into the toy bag of a little kid,
their large windows with panes staring at me in
curiosity,
I'm a tailor who cuts out clouds.

All right! But where are your stars, Amsterdam?

I'll come back to you with tons of them
attaching each of them to each of your curls.
Don't forget, Amsterdam is the city of yellow street-cars
and tulips,
you're my darling now!

A face I seem to recognize is shaking my hand:

Van Gogh, my old friend, with a red beard and a
chopped ear.
Hello! The man who paints the landscapes with winds
and fires;
God's twin brother, the devil of colors.

A dark blue rain is falling over Paris.
A dark blue tango is on my lips.
La Seine is my despondent maiden.
A gossamer curtain stretched over
the Earth, there you have Paris.

I want to write a blue letter home;
a dark blue poem… every word of it smelling of
cinnamon;
let a sea breeze sweep off the 'a' s ; let the poem have no
'a' s in it.
But my salted vagabondage must remain

with my glass of raki.

Goodbye Berlin, I'll Be Back Again

To Prof. Server Tanilli

A woman is washing her red lips with raki
in the most erotic hours of the night.
She is peering so darkly into my eyes that
I'd make her screech like a bird
if I were to clasped her in my arms.

Another glass of raki please, Gültekin!
My heart of forty will fail otherwise.

I wonder if the moon and the stars are frozen;
this is not the end of the space.
Enough of this coyness,
come Berlin, come and sit by my side,
I'm the only one that can warm you up.

When are they closing this tavern Turan,
in the early hours of the morning? What time *is* morning
by the way?
Let the person who burnt these violet spleens come
forth,
Mümtaz is already in the raki glasses.

2.
Prof Server's account of Young Turks:
reclining on the divan is a German lady
with lips wet and
breasts quivering gently

Come, Enver Pasha, don't click your heels,
Do it, for God's sake!

Clumsy in politics

95

Clumsy in sex are
These Young Turks.
They had the funny idea
of governing the State
by clicking heels;
and they failed to do it!

Night is snowy and cold
Turkey is so distant like stars afar
A red rose radiates from my mouth
Amorous advances in our eyes
Prof Server and I

We've captured Berlin.

The Stockholm Symphony

My heart the source of distress,
What can rescue you from it
in a morning under the snow of Stockholm?

I'm watching
dejected and with some anguish
at the skiing men
over the icy hills and dales.
In the narrow streets of İzmir ending up at sea
My youth with acacias crowned
Snows
In my mind's eye.
Life under whose roof I had exchanged kisses
With a refined vagary and friendship,

with a glorious spleen
I've caught you up.

My life is the life of a poem hunter.

The deer shepherds of the North
Are dancing to the accompaniment
Of thousand year old ballads
under the nocturnal sun
Hanging from the sky like a purple lantern.
on the Baltic Mother
A Swedish woman is strolling in the morning
With her lap dog.
A blonde man is hunting fish in their sleep
Drilling the pack of ice with a steel drill
The pack of ice on which he stands
smoking a Havana cigar,
while his dog frolics with the fish he had caught.

This year also the spring was late in Sweden
under the thawing snow;
like a kid's shriek of joy
It will pop out from the wood
reviving
a tiny daisy.
The tiny daisy will rise its head
to challenge the world.
Allied with its companions,
they will paint the Earth in yellow.
Vapors will rise to the heights
from the soft belly of the Earth divinity

Just as every life
Just as every forest
has a poem of its own,
so has every poem a life.
I have no one
but my poetry anyway;
I'm a hunter of poems
a spleen hunter.

I wonder if my hands
are a pair of doves
or
a couple of daggers?

The wet spring is nigh
with its dancing flowers
heralding the advent of SUMMER.

From the wet lakes of the North,
from its dark forests
blondes with firm breasts

will come from the heights down to Stockholm
with their golden hairs braided
like the Viking women,
of thousands of years ago.

They will remove their dresses
in the streets of the city ablaze
under the heat of June
Even tough you pour over me
100.000 lakes of Sweden
you cannot extinguish
the wick of my heart.

What have I been doing all these years,
other than opening a gateway to love and hope?
Lining up the words of verses like tiny bombs
With the joy of a boy that pricks with a needle
the colored balloons
blowing up the 'fields of sorrow'
and renting asunder the pyramid of pains
to find out new paths opening to the world…

Who knows what one cannot find
in an evening while gazing at the sea,
as one listens to the music of a fiddle!
Can you throw away
whatever you have experienced in life,
while fluttering like a wounded bird
in the blue shoreline of nostalgia?
Can you confront life
like a shrill
cry
of a newborn?

O! the number of things we forget

in between the lines
of a letter to a friend!
We are unloading vats of
brandy, rum and oranges coming from Spain.
The drunkard sailors
are shivering from cold,
aboard the deck.
Having collected the
yellow spleen
from the yellow brandy bottles
I am writing the first lines of this symphony.
To collect a spleen
unknown
from the valleys of sorrow;
and like the claws of a tiger
mount them on life's peaks.
This may be the beginning of poetry perhaps.

A dock laborer
in a voice reminiscent of a saxophone
is reciting poems by Nazım, the old man;
O my country!
O my country!
O my country!
Even though it is in Finnish
Even though it is in Chinese
Even though in the Aztec tongue,
that makes no difference;
For Nazım, the old man,
is
the father
of all peoples
of all tongues

If you're going to become

a poem hunter,
young man!
If you're going to give birth
to words,
young woman!
You've got to hunt down yourself first;
and have others' scan
the lineaments of sorrow
in history's rivers.

EVERY NEW DAY
SHALL BE THE CAPITAL
OF SORROW.

My Approach To The World Is A Dark Blue Tango

Man gave birth to cities,
then cities to men;
What else may have traced the map
of the human heart if not afflictions?

Poetry, our common son,
is both the son of history and of the public.
This is why he looks sideways at the world;
not even military trucks could smash it.

Although spleen
is history's sister,
it is as old as history itself,
only bluer.

Poetry is bluer than blue.
Therefore spleen envies poetry.
I put down one and carry
a yellow autumn and me
are equal to Boreas.

Only rains can wound me
so can history.
Like a yellow plum
my looks fall down.

I've received an envelope
with corners decorated with roses
it contains a photograph of mine
winds decorate its edges.

The poet's heart does not lay in ambush;
it is in the open.

Even though vultures may attack it
his heart can shake the world entire.

When I enter a poem hope regenerates;
For, it is well known that
my approach to the world
is a dark blue tango.

Scorch My Face With Istanbul Rakis

Having exchanged kisses
and fists
with Istanbul rakis
the summer of '87
had been a raging conflagration
where my tender heart was
like a fern.
Even after having stretched my heart
over the waters of the Bosphorus
Look! I'm parading before you!
In my lips
that the seagulls screeches
smeared with blood
a world
bloody and salted
conceals me.
Scorch my face
with Istanbul rakis
add to it that wry spleen
of the Hungarian films.
If I am a passenger
whose baggage is stuffed
with poems and winds,
with rivers and terraces,
I risk being shot of course
in a stone paved courtyard
with roof over it bedecked with stars;
Bach's concertos to be my coffin.
Telephones, stars and rivers
that interconnect cities,
sly looks
and cold white wine
sweep me off.

Well! Who may I be,
I whose face
is scorched to vie with Beirut.

-A pigeon is reported to have pierced the world?

Messenger of gentle looks
a crazy fall
gushes out
from my veins.

If I am summing up my drunken nights
like match sticks
spilled on the ground
if the fall ruthlessly
unbuttons
the first buttons
of the white blouses of young maidens,
we must inquire then:

-who is the first customer of love?

Look! How frantically stretches
itself
that white marble
to catch
the orange leaf
fluttering in the air.

The first snow fell
tonight in Stockholm.
The night
was as beautiful
as the first snow;

reanimating the green statues
of the city,
dampening
a thin and long
smarting pain
as though roving in the olive groves of the Aegean
I strolled in parks and subways
having difficulty though to force my bo
into the narrow streets of the city
exchanging kisses with the clouds
I thought: this city
Full of lights and sounds
is my answer to the
world.

Words are my bench.
My voice
grows in volume
with human voices.
I drank till the early hours of the morning
with a migrant worker
whose heart was aflame
with longing for his beloved
he had left behind the mountains.
As the sun undid the dark seams
of the night
with its bright days,
in each of our goblets had
fallen a field of orchids.
O little darling,
the queen of snow capped mountains
spleen executed by shooting
you
me
and all of us?

O! Those Mediterranean Cities

O those Mediterranean cities
hanging down from the stars
dangling in the night.

Barcelona thrown into the Mediterranean
a blue abyss;
Mersin don't forget darling
you're the most beautiful girl of the Mediterranean.

Never ask about Bodrum:
You can never tell where it will stay overnight,
it will flirt with the Mediterranean
while making love with the Aegean
in the meantime waiting for her husband's
return from Venice.

Whenever I swim in the Mediterranean
cities brushes against
My hands and feet.
Their streets are poured into the sea,;
come on gather them together
if you can
all through the night

Am I Looking For A Street To Get Engaged

A kid
is selling a roll at Bebek
with pockets full of acacias.
His mother thrashed everyday by his father.

I am roaming in New York,
why, I don't know,
wearing a light green shirt
-Can it be that I am looking for street to get engaged?

The blade of a guillotine falls on us
dividing the evening into two.
Wherever we my turn our gaze
on one side is Bebek on the other Manhattan.

The fall is taking our picture!

-Why not, buddy?

I Am Not A Fighter But A Rose Grower

There! The spring is in once again;
my hair exposed to winds,
hail! I say to the Earth where I'm in exile;
Hail! The home
of insects, volcanoes, winds and oceans.
Our little garden,
the planet where I was born,
I am looking at the calendar: it's March,
yet I am hit against April.
If you want to know the name of the beauty
with whom I exchange kisses, it's May.
It was I who had planted the rose bushes
flirting now with stars.
For I am not a fighter but a rose grower.

I am strolling on
the frozen northern sea.
Drilling the ice with their steel drills
the Swedes hunt fish in a state of sleep.
The March sun, stretching its hand out from
half open clouds, pulls our hair:
over my head hover 'dark thoughts' about the world;
I am afraid of man's ferocity,
Of weapons,
wars and religions…

If one day I lose
all hope from 'human' beings,
bury me in this poem;
for, I am not a fighter but a rose grower.

Do you know another planet
smelling of tea and apples?

Are you the master of
volcanoes and rainbows? No!
You're but a passing visitor upon this Earth
with a return ticket in your pocket.
You'll be kissed by God some day
on an abyss.
There's a city among the clouds, there
shall you go.
I happen to be a tiny cell of nature, brother to
ants, butterflies, trees, stars and waters.

'G' stands for the gullet of the city
'e' is more feminine that 'a'
'C' can not be any one else than Cemal Süreyya.
'I' ? Who is he?
-Ilhan Berk, surely
Making his rounds at Bodrum
in his car of poems.
carrying in his pocket 'Fields of words.'
K. known to everybody : Kerim
my son
the handsomest of all the lads in the world
13 years old
abandoned tennis
to write criticisms on books
Salihli is the district,
where the mountains are purple
must be blossoming now
in clusters.
In the International Fair of İzmir
sailors are strolling with lilacs on their heads
instead ordinary caps;
high school girls
chatter about their boyfriends...
There! A kiss out of the blue

110

hardly ever to be forgotten
coy
and
fugitive.

I have a secret date
with a pigeon, its back buried
in the valley: our house
is a dried river bed
the evening becomes color of rose
as we exchange kisses.
O the sunset!
It's a plot anyhow;
while love is to get enrolled to life
You know what you should do? Just go!
Befriend a mountain range,
stand trial with the birds!

For, a bird
does not move aside its voice
to avoid colliding with the spring.

There! Spring again;
my hair exposed to the winds,
Hail I say to the Earth
where I am but an exile.

It was I who had planted the rose bushes
flirting now with stars.
For I am not a fighter but a grower of roses.

Sanem

Two black olive seeds
are my daughter's eyes
two nests of nostalgia

Aegean black plains
Are your wedding dress
the clouds are your veil

Olive trees are dancing
And rivers are singing for you
My heart overflows with pain
over brimming my banks

I'll cry for you every day
as long as I live
my dearest, my beauty
my Sanem

Two black olive seeds
are my daughter's eyes
two nests of nostalgia
the poppy field of my heart

I'll cry for you every day
as long as I live

Notes Of An Earthling (1)

I carried my address book to Beijing
On it are sleeping
the children of a water-melon seller. The night
is like black velvet
swaying on your eyelashes.
I am always far away anyhow
On the streets between Naples and Rio.
I am listening to what the stones
have been recounting for a million years.
My first friends was an apple orchard
that once was the bottom of the sea.
And I was tiny earthling
staying under the wings of the birds.
There used to be a park here
with newly painted swings
and a shy girl with small breasts
smelling of fresh green almonds...

Beijing! It smells of soup every morning.
Millions of bike riders
sticking to the clouds, to the park.
A fisherman's net is straightening up
to avoid being mixed up with meridians
The Chinese Wall is a gigantic kite
sleeping cuddled up on the mountains
I am always far away anyhow
in a tavern between Beijing and İzmir.
I am flirting with Chinese girls.
I am flirting with the trails
one day they will get me for sure.

Ah! One thing or other ends each day.
A love affair ends, joys end...

113

Youngsters dance between
Between he jaws of the jackals.
As for me, I am always far away
For a water-melon seller from Beijing
for a poet from Naples
I describe an inlet of Halikarnassos
At dawn I ride a pitch dark pony
My face is filtered through a blue violet.
On my shoulder linger the bites
of betrothed maidens
That I take shelter behind a city is not in vain
The iodine on my wounds
Is not vain.
The birds need no persuading to sing.
I know it: t h e y   a r e   a f t e r   m e.
When morning enters the city
like a yellow cavalryman
they no doubt will get me:

-Hey earthling! We have found the traces of your heart.

So, here I am right in front of you
on a pitch black pony
a wild orchid on my collar.

Notes Of An Earthling (2)

My address book is afloat now in the Atlantic ocean
surmounted by volcanoes
and an old album whose photos are all
dispersed on the surface of the sea.
My face stretched between
Lake Van
and the Atlantic Ocean
scarred by a jack knife:
birds are flying through it.
Everybody knows where I am
the opium I eat in a word
the dawn at which we had been caught red-handed
while fornicating in Borneo with gypsies from the sea
are known to everybody. When I, like an '*efe* dancer'
struck my knee on the mountains,
clouds are were blown into in smithereens on my
shoulders.
my last refuge is the orchard
trying to catch
a ship that had weighed anchor.

I know I am being tracked;
they'll get me sooner or later;
blindfolded, not with a band
but with the chirping of birds
in between my lips rotating
a thorny rose stem.

My address book is now afloat now on the Black Sea.
In a city concealed
from the world.
Tchekov's looking through the window
of his house flooded with moonlight

on the Primorsky Boulevard in Odessa.
A baby carriage
is kept falling
down the well-known stairs of the Battleship Potemkin;
Pushkin is dueling with cups of brandy
at the bar of the Londonskaya Hotel
teen age girls in the street
prostituting themselves to 'westerners',
the choice Odessa champagne in their hands; time
is perched on the window sill
is like a flower pot in Odessa

They have handcuffed my address book
to a Gondola In Venice;
In it were discovered the forbidden plum trees
and Mondays turned yellow.
Penguins entered my poems riding streetcars
How can Penguins
ever enter my poem: it's incomprehensible;
incomprehensible
are the tales told.
by the little spinning wheel
on a mountain village.

I know I being tracked
I'll get caught sooner or later

-O the earthling! We've tracked your heart down!

Look! I'm standing before you
A pitch dark mare
under me
patches of dark clouds
spread on my knees
on my lapel

is a wild
ORCHID

Notes Of An Earthling (3)

My address book is detained in Sweden.
Reindeers are rushing about
in the snow covered valleys.
I'm naming time
with a forest that shakes itself.
Birds' fluttering
makes me nearer to the world.
My face squeezed
between buses and seas
makes my countenance i l l e g i b l e.
I had been here long before.
I was encircled
by a river as a belt.
I caught fish
with my stone axe.
The warmth of my hand is
still on the caverns walls.

I am wanted ever since.

I know
I'll be caught sooner or later
with ivy shall my hands
be tied up.

We are all detained by certain things
in each of us
meander narrow streets
and the balconies of our youth exposed to rains
O my youth! Flown away.
What's dripping from our heart
not is blood
but leaves of rose

color of champagne.

My algebra teacher,
from whom I always got zero
my beloved in the primary school,
and my chum Ahmet,
you've stepped
in the garden of this poem
Welcome!

Everybody knows where I am
I'm the first customer of the sun in Paris;
I may also have company of a Lisbon morning
My body
floating in blood
drained in Saxophone sounds.
I'm riding a pitch dark mare
with dawn as cap on my head
I'm vying
with a spleen tasting liquor.

I know I am WANTED wherever I go
sooner or later I'm doomed to be caught.

O Earthling! We've found out
the trace of your heart.

Here I am!
When you see me
I am waiting for you
on the mountains
stripped of their white shirts;
on my lapel
a wild
ORCHID

I Am Duelling With the River

Good morning sadness! The blue cloud
hiding in my coffin
Let them take you out and show around
when they kill me
behind a yellow ocean
You go to the movies. Do go!
Get engaged, if you like,
iron your shirt, listen to the news,
watch the corpses of children
falling in the middle of your room
from your colour TV
Light your stove
with machine gun fire in Bosnia

You are not in Bosnia
You are in New York or Istanbul
I don't know
where I am
who I am with
and when
who are my face and my hands with?
Am I drinking beer
inside the stomach of a whale?
Among the opera buildings and parks;
Maybe I am wounded like a diver
suffering from decompression sickness
blood running all over my face;
Bird shops
in the Las Ramblas boulevard
in Barcelona
Spanish girls
whose hair falling down to their hips
the portrait

a street painter did for me in Rome
do they redeem anything?

As I get to know more
I have less to say
Why are we? And why does the world exist?
My jacket is riddled with holes
I am wandering here and there
carrying swallows and missiles

One day we are all going to die
insects will eat
our penises and our heart

Our faces will shine
under the earth
like a mirror
I don't know you but
I am not going to take off my glasses
to see the worms and rains better
You too take a comb
to comb your hair
If you ask me: "Everyone should have his statue
made of marble"

When they put in the museum
our cold faces
let's not smile before the tourists come!
- haven't they already paid for their tickets!
You can carve everyone's face out of marble
but it's another matter to engrave
the faces of prophets
Because their faces
are as gentle as bird songs

Everyone likes something:
maybe you like prophets
but I like orchids
and women
Kursat causes the best fight at bars
by nailing into the night
the raki glass in his hand
The elder brother of Turkish language is Cemal Sureya
Who gives the order to the sky to rain:
Necati Doluorman in Izmir

the negatives of life in his pocket
Mehmet H. Dogan beats up the street singers
who rape the young Izmir night
and a glass of raki drunk with pleasure
by playing arabesgue music.
Galip Akcali
banishes himself
under the orange trees in Bodrum.
Ahmet Necdet in Izmir Cukuru
in any bar he goes to
akes out of his pocket
either his poems or the Enlightenment

Everyone likes something:
Mr Jesus used to like nails
Mr Mohammed his wives
My lover Leyla from primary school!
Now a mother with three children in Kalamis
used to like so much
holding my penis in arithmetic lessons

Life is like a revolving wheel at a fun fair
What is that which they call "heaven"?
Land for sale, child!

If we collect bottle lids,
red ones, one paper-bag full,
would uncle God like us
maybe he would allow us to ride on his bicycle.
- Cemal!!! Are the girls alright there?

You go to the marketplace: How nice!
You've filled up your bag with bargains
You have your coal and wood supply for winter as well
A cup of tea in your hand
you're looking at the nude and bloody picture
of a dead woman on the newspaper,
who committed suicide with her child
People were burnt alive in Sivas: you remain silent!
You haven't even read a line
from Metin
from Asim!

Juntas have come and passed: you remained silent!
Be silent, Mr, be silent! You were never born!
You!
were
never
born ...

A Bosnian child
is looking for his leg
ripped off by shrapnel
- Have you seen it?

What have we witnessed, the great stream?
The big brother
which came down to us
by flowing through the white bellies
of the fish and the stars

123

of Caesar and Cleopatra!
The eternal and blue hour of the Universe
The rain inside a bird!

- What have we witnessed with you?
We have witnessed the cities and rivers
hanged by spears

Stockholm:
the city fluttering
between blue towers and canals
She awakens below the snow
with the smell of hot, fresh coffee
I reach out every morning
and steal a few lines
from the waters of the Bosphorus
Or I dig out a time-worn sadness
deep in the coral shores of Foca
Is it any different
drinking tea in Van
than looking across the Bosphorus
in Istanbul
If you're not in love
the Sea won't kiss you
- What time is it? What an absurd question

Are we playing hide-and-seek with Napoleon?
Who destroyed the Berlin Wall? Birds?
Dictators assemble for parade in our era: one by one
they go into the debris of History
I think we're going to leave
our big ordeals behind
and see the coming of a good century
my friends...
And I - if I live -

in the year 2000
will ride on the World again
and continue to give out poems
as an old poet

Books, yellow roses
and rivers as well go sightseeing
They do their jackets in yellow tramcars
Nobody has taught them
how to sing: they stay contemplative
They had learnt in primary school
how to splash their feet
in the sea

You all know it: a terrace is not
a guillotine
nor is a steppe a cloud
A bird doesn't catch a train
but window shutters always tap
against the Taurus mountains
You've shot your gun
but why
do you drink your arsenic without milk?
- What did you study in primary school?

- Did you study Barbaros Hayrettin Pasa,
Gulliver, Robinson Crusoe? Pekosbil?
Uncle Barbaros!
Uncle with his hat made of winds!
When we last drunk red wine
with silver cups
the fish didn't eat your blue beard
in the Mediterrenean Sea
I was a young pirate then
combing his hair with rum

An Italian beauty
With shivering hips like the sea
raped me for 7 days and 7 nights
on a gold plated bedstead

why friends Pekosbil and Jane Calamity
they've come and rode on acacia trees
they've got the spring engaged
with a snow-white bison
we are going to smoke the peace pipe
with our Indian brothers and sisters
before the northerners in blue uniforms
open up their stomachs with their long knive

Dr Whitman was found ice dead
in the North Pole - after 100 years -
Under a photogenic light
he had written these last lines
on his notebook:

- There is no grass here but
there are nice Eskimo girls

I am in the Far East in a Chinese boutique
Behind the counter an old Chinaman sells
smoked sea snakes, mussels dead eagles, small trees
and handcarts
A green Budha statue
is looking at History secretly
through a keyhole
Fish who have caught cold
are riding on bicyles

Ants are wandering in cadillacs

I shake hands
with a crocodile
who has just
finished his breakfast

The Chinaman's voice comes from deep in the cosmos:
- Mr! he says, here are our queens
French, English, Japanese, Arab
Their necks are so thin like a decanter
Cut under the
G UILLOTINE

-Which one would you like?

His 13 year old daughter shouts from the kitchen:
- Please! Tell me, dad,
how would I make the soup
without killing the tortoise?

The white dove
having rearranged her glasses
is picking with her beak
the little pink papers
from the "board of luck and good fortune":

There is no forest in Iceland
And Indians don't have beards

Casanova used to drink chocolate
not champagne

What would happen
if Havva (Eve) bit the snake
instead of the apple?

The Chinese wear white
in times of death: in China
the colour of pain is white

Rilke and Orhan Veli
two wizards
drink raki in the meyhane of Kaptan
looking across the Bosphorus

Every night
how can you become Mongolian, Zuhtu?

The coffin of each star
is a black hole in the space

How can you cut
an ant's head on the guillotine?
This is not a question
it's a puff up

A Japanese prime minister rules Peru
What about our hearts?
Who is ruling our hearts?

The police arrested Rimbaud
after they caught him in an indecent act with his poems

I am sleeping on a cloud
Pass me slowly underneath

"Human beings: what a pity?" said
Augusti Strindberg

An Islandic beauty gushes out from my saxophone

You've gone to the marketplace: how nice!
You've filled up your bag cheaply: how nice!
You got married and had children: how nice!
A Bosnian child
is looking for his leg
ripped off by shrapnel
- Was it you who sold it to the butcher?

In Barcelona
I am putting my feet in the sea
My feet touch a woman's foot
in Antalya
If we didn't have our feet
we would have fallen from the earth
and maybe our shirts would have got tangled
in the stars and
we would have remained suspended
in the air
Whenever I go to Izmir
I collect my first poems from the streets
My heart comes under missile fire
of an old and painful love
In my pocket a notebook
with previous convictions
full of new poems
so many addresses I have

If you want
take my photos again
with the sounds of rain
Mount me on your hips
tossing about like the sea
put a blue lake on our bed
instead of a sheet

Ah Nile! All of us were made
out of your mud
You,
You kiss with desert winds
in December
that's why
your grey waves become a pink fire
Birds and pharocks make love on you

What is that which ill-treats me
in the river Nile or in an Egean city?
What is that which saddens me?
The little child who sells flowers in Eminonu shouts:

-Today violets are so full of it!

Dionysos discovered wine
by squeezing grapes in his hands
Goya, the master of colours
drew his first patterns with coal
The ear which Van Gogh cut and wrap inside a towel
is listening to us...
That big ear that hears infinitely everything!
A convicted and nomad child inside me:

I a m duelling wit h a river.

What Time Is It On The Earth?

My face
fluttering like a flag in the wind
in a gondola in Venice.

The smell
of vineyards on my shirt
light blue;
when I was being smuggled to
modern and cities in distress
I had not glanced
at my watch.

Whereas
morning is
the greatest smuggler
It buries,
its guilt charged
on the shoulders of a blue abyss
saved during the night
in the Atlantic Ocean

A melancholy train station
in the depths
of my heart
where I descend by an elevator.
What is a defunct love
that a defunct love has kindled?
Who introduced me to the poppies?
Into whichever city I wander
my greatest guilt
is to live
adjacent to the world.
In the street wherein the night is longest

I scorched my hair
with newspapers
and rakis.

I am choosing the wind
that will take me
to somewhere;
for, winds are flying staircases;
its steps
gateways to cities.

What's that
that everybody knows?
When does the sea
becomes immeasurably immense?

And while
my face waves to and fro
a gondola
What time is it
this morning in the world?

Poetry Clips My Wings At The Edge Of Precipices

Astride on the sound of saxophone
July
makes a start with the rough sketch
of a new love

July
that befits mostly stained cities.
whenever he takes off his cap
he is the
first child
shot down in the orchards

I'm taking off the rose with its stem attached to my
flannel
What's the name of the rose?
Who could ever tell?
Who looks where?
Who sees what?

Open air movies, jazz melodies
my face
riddled with a ball-point pen
how is it to be transported
to overseas?

What have I inherited
from my raider forbears
except
my cheekbones?

I'll go off taking my dark blue voice with me
from summer cities tumbled over
not being deceived by

seagulls and ice ream sellers
wearing a starched shirt whose collars
may
any time now
explode.

Recently elderly uncles and aunts
a people with hair and jackets burnt
were deceived by the world
aboard Marmara.
Who they love Heavens knows
And
under his eyelids
crashed is
Istanbul.

It may be that
what they are after
is a
white and visionary
life.
Everybody knows it
Love
is a scuffle in a backstreet
with the ocean.

What do we need?
A village in the middle of the Atlantic Ocean;
El Golfo.
Elder brother of Foça
is arching its back
like a white cat
flanked by a volcano and seagull shrieks.

A tiny cloud
is in search for
its brother
above
Lake Van
For a couple of quick ones
at a pub.

Astride on a sound of saxophone
Between Tauruses and Arizona
O the evening
that slashed at my face!
where
shall we meet?

As the full moon as
bright as a jack knife
I say
that it is the poetry
that clips my wings at the edge of precipices.

Summer Scenes From '97 Fairy Chimneys And Unaging Friendships

My Face
airborne
above the fairy chimneys
of Cappadocia;
the fairy chimneys,
progeny of
The Erciyes and Hasan mountains,
never take off their hats
but have been waiting for the sun
to set
these millions of years
in the Red Valley

In Sweden.
on the shore of Lake Vettern,
Grenna,
hardly a town
perhaps a caramel;
It received its hue
from the rose breasts of maidens.

In Çanakkale
at the Lapseki Şen district
smart Ahmet
a virtuoso of clarinets.
Renowned for permeating the balconies
with sad airs.

In Bursa,
at Şükrü the Arab's
a glass of rakı
will shake
all your being.
and let the mountains
be crowned with clouds.
Let's drink pals
and let the sun in the horizon
topple over into our glasses.

All the streets of the Earth
have been transported by tourists
to Foça.
A confusion in the world map.
No fees are quoted
on the THY price list
for carriage of street fragments.

Lake Sapanca
surrounded by mountains
with misty eyes
connect our hearts to
the most beautiful mornings while
young men hunt wild geese
with double-barreled guns.

Eğridir
a small township
but can vie with Bodrum and Antalya
across Lake Eğridir
a queen
never been a like

137

in the world.
With a slight shift to the west
all the Aegean islands
is sure to die
from jealousy.

In Sweden
midsummer festivities;
cities have been evacuated
The Swedes
gorge themselves with herrings
boiled potatoes, hard bread
plus
strawberries in their red shacks
and drink
aquavit
So green becomes Sweden
in July
Shake any branch you like
your hair will be assailed
by a lake.

The Salt Lake
grazed my face
my bus is buried
in a wheat field.
Carriages
carrying lemons
pass by me
Hey driver!
What do your lemons conceal?

In Izmit
did an armed detachment
confiscate this poem
digging a tunnel through the lines
headed by
Suat Özdemir
Poetry's bluest guy
accompanied by
sharp marksmen of images
Nilüfer, Yasemin, Çiğdem, Kayhan and Alaattin
who snatched this poem boarding a train
a cloud of laughter fell next to the machinist;
you may assert that clouds have no names,
you are wrong, Sir: Look there you have Baha Koçak.
Ruhan Odabaş
Is carrying on is back a load of Laz anecdotes.
Tell me now who carries what?
Ruhan the load
or the load Ruhan?

Ruşen Hakkı
who without a wink
burnt his heart
among words.
and has washed the human face
in oceans
these 45 years.
His poems became bridges that connect
us to each other.
Regardless of the street you take in İzmit
its name is
Ruşen Hakkı.

12.

O the blue fish of Marmara!
Beware of Yavuz Bey! He scares them so much;
for they know
that if they to fall
into the porcelain plate of the doctor
They will immediately undergo
transplantation
each of their bones being
sucked and eyes carved.

Fethiye
has convened all the tourists of the world,
and repudiates all criticism of its township.
It has learned indeed how to prepare
the schwarzwald for tourists.
The sea shore is crammed with
coffee-houses, ice cream sellers, boot blacks
diffident newly married couples
philanderers in search for a prey
hungry but proud dogs.
Boats making preparations for their night journeys
in pursuit of moonlight
designed for Tourists.

In Lake Köyceğiz
nature pounces upon us
through rushes
nobody can escape anyhow
either nature
or poetry.

Büyükada
riding in a phaeton
driven
by roses;
Burgaz
its sister
astern our ship
beats the Marmara sea with its feet.

Seat of pleasure in the Muğla plateau
Nay, more than a seat;
space ship docked under
an age old plane tree.
Süreyya Baba
removes a piece from it to fabricate a bird.
That's why houses of Muğla have assumed the shape of
a bird
and fly away certain evenings.
Only the birdman Süreyya baba
knows where they go.

In Pendik
the Kastamonu cake
has topped all other cakes.
but acts modestly toward the pie.
The salon is packed with
soldiers, peasant women
laborers and poets.
On one side of our mouth is a cake
on the other a pie.
A high school girl
in the arms of her boyfriend
as though in the midst of a field of poppies
is crying.
Aha!

How charmingly
she is crying.
What do I care for the Kastamonu cake
or for any pie anyhow

The Pendik landing stage
is about to collapse
as though snatched from an old movie
squinting at the Pavli island
furtively.
An eminent poet has mislaid his eyes on the Island:
Nazım Hikmet.
Nobody passes by him
without butting up his jacket.

In Burgaz
Sait Faik is waiting for us.
At our table sea-bass
as fresh as a maiden's breast.
Seagulls fill up our glasses.
Melike, Mazlum, Bora and I
we are at the horizon of an evening of no return.
Right, but why
does Bora Ayanoğlu prefer brandy to raki?
What's that showering on us Sait Bey?
is it rain or raki?

Evening news on the
Swedish radio read by Osman İkiz and Hasan Özkaya:
The police are in pursuit of the sun smuggled
somewhere
in Stockholm.

According to the latest weather forecast
it has been arrested,
being caught in flagrante delicto
while trying to break in
a maiden's blouse;
detained now and hand-cuffed
at the police headquarters
No severe injuries!

Yes
the '97 scenes end here
esteemed reader.
Leaving
'All alone'
Özkan Mert
go to another address
from whose pen
drop
fairy chimneys, blue fish, green lemons and lakes
and friendship ever green!

Love Poems

For 'E'

Whenever I look into your eyes
my heart is washed in an ocean;
Wherever I go I remain with you
Just like the stars in heaven.

I've traced you on a raindrop
by that lake's shore
your first kiss you bestowed on me...
The tip of my umbrella was piercing the clouds.

The point we stare at has no end
You'll always be the moonlight asleep in my hair,
a warm stream gently flowing by my shoulders.

And the most beautiful declaration of love
ejected from your lips color of dawn
will never be obliterated;
I dare not wash my hands
lest the scent of your hands evaporate.

2.

Your kiss dear is as beautiful as a spring morn
and as light as a butter-fly,
whereas I am but a mountain hut
on which your kisses are planted.

Whenever we make love
the night assumes the color of your eyes;
Whenever I kiss your lips
my heart hanging on the stars sways to and fro.

You look so beautiful
with your eyes fixed on me;
with your curvaceous shoulders,
the flutter of birds' wings assumes your name.

Your attitude to me?
How can I depict it;
for, we're henceforth one upon the Earth.

If I kiss the palm of your hand
violets bloom in them;
and your back, whenever I kiss it,
I get lost in a white cloud.

Making love with you
is to dismount the birds' chirping
in order to straddle the clouds.

3.

The small lips of my beloved taste of cherry.
Each of us thinks of the other twenty four hours a day.
And when we do come together we make nonstop love.
In the words of Cemal Süreyya: never seen the like of it!
On a bright sunny day
your eyes are full of bliss
like the raindrops falling down dancing
upon the Earth .

4.

I kiss each of your fingers
included the little one;
you clutch me like a plum
clutching on its seed.
There, you neither need air nor light.
I drink your skin
as though it were water.

Your skin is my planet.

I Slept In The Streets Of Warsaw In The Open Air With Birds

Love is a clumsy thing
like the birds getting ready for their first flight
in July.
Once the summer is over! Farewell to love, they say.
The summer is not over, it just falls down!
You'll be dallying with your heart;
for love is unavoidable.
Ride your bicycle! I *am* riding it. Kiss the sky, I am
kissing it.
I went on, followed by butter-flies, ice cream sellers
and deck chairs in my pursuit,
I passed by the summer cities toppled over.
I asked: how can I taper a river with my jack knife?
I asked: how can I taper a word with my jack knife
so that the point may rent the ocean asunder?

Who was standing as candidate for deltas this summer?
On whose door hangs the bluest of mountains? The
summer!
Pity it is a *zeybek* in the Aegean,
with knees buried in clouds;
his dagger
thrust into mountains,
where there is a scent of violet
there his house is.

Into the waters emptying in Lake Van
the gray-mullet lays its eggs in May
Your face gets immersed into the poem in the Black Sea
plateaus
The fields between Gümüşhane and Bayburt
are not fields but butterflies;
they flutter

at the tips of the sun's rays.

In Krakow, the greatest square of the Middle Ages
At Rynek Glowy, Polish girls saunter in the night
their beautiful legs snow-white.
The river Wisla runs slowly across the city;
throwing blue roses to the square
maidens bending to pick them up;
it can't fail kissing their legs.
Clumsy are the birds
getting ready for their first flight in July;
No matter what you do,
a spelling mistake is inevitable
during the last loves in July.
You may go to sleep with birds in the streets
in Warsaw, if you like;
or load your heart
on a blue mountain
the last July of the millennium is at an end
like a jack knife in your pocket
with a radiant love

Spring is The Bride of Cities

A city cannot know itself;
it avidly waits for the spring
learns its name from rivers
and wheat fields
the spring is its bride
of all cities; like
a timid child
hides in parks.
Regardless which is the mountain
It makes love with
It lets fall like a rose
The evening
Upon the earth.
I gathered cherries today,
ate ice cream;
my heart beaten over and over again
I forgot everything!
I wonder under which meridian has
my face remained handsome.
May
is the month in which I let people fondle me
July!
The highwayman that confronts me
With a pungent odor of carnation
I am wet throughout in April
either from rain from love
or from both of them

My Heart Posing For The World

Today I listened to the thawing snow.
I exchanged kisses with a field
chocolate colour
renting the sky I fought the clouds
that strayed toward the world.

I know, it's April
in which winds gently blow
lashing our hair against the mountains
and making one drunk as though
one has been drinking all day.
I, who was squeezed between April and the clouds,
a blonde cutie has just passed by
making my heart leap from its cage and
posing for the world!

So Many Beautiful Things In The World

1.

There are so many beautiful things in the world.
For instance, I know a street in İzmir which flows
into the sea as though pearls were spilling on the floor.
The sleepy streets in Equador, in the city of Quito,
when they go mad climb over the mountains.

And the evening falls red on those mountains.

On the rivers flowing in the depths of Amazon
a snow-white orchid grows!
So sweet and pungent is its odor that
it makes one gallop like a crazy mare
on the shore of one's heart.

Our heart is the looking-glass of flowers.

They say that only the China Wall is seen
when looked down from the moon; that's not true.
I looked and saw simply
a poppy on the Palandöken heights
and a couple of butter-flies
making love in the air..

2.

O the number of bridges I have known!
I'm sure you know them as well: The Bosphorus Bridge
for instance!
at its leisure hours during the night it hunts stars as a
diversion.
How it suffers from human beings in the course of the
day
and from the seagulls that keep on hitting against it.
I know it will move away one day,
only God knows where exactly.

Nowhere else would it become save the Bosphorus.

O the number of cities I have known!
With breasts jutting out from their bras
wake up in the morning like young girls,
exchanging kisses with the first rays of the sun
blooming like red roses upon the Earth

Each city opens to a new city from one of its extremities.

O the number of poets like fire I have known: Rimbaud
for one
who had written the *Bateau Ivre* without having seen the
sea before
and washed his words in the oceans of life.

O the number of pretty women in the world
brunettes, blondes, color of chocolate
each more beautiful and attractive than the other
on their tight and soft skin
Empires had been founded, empires had collapsed;
their single kiss triggered revolutions;
had it not been for women and love

would it be worth to live upon the Earth?
To whom would we be reciting this poem if not to them?
By the way, I have a paramour;
a world beauty,
whenever I look into her eyes
I feel like falling over the stars
even though I may be clasping
the Earth with all my might.

What have fascinated me have been these beauties.

4.
O poet, with beautiful words and magic words
you deceive my servants, says God Almighty;
have I created only beautiful things,
have I not also generated wars, deaths, separations?

Sure you have, God! You can settle your account
with them in that respect.
I, for my part, have created only good things
without waiting in return any reward from my fellow
brethren
merely to make them happy in read them.
If this is an offense,
I am ready to be
fuel in your hell!

The rationale of or Apologia for the recovery of my Red Pelerine mentioned in a footnote in a book which i hunted out at second hand book market prior to cosmic pollution caused by pigeons which had perched on who took wolfgang Amadeus Mozart, Pomegranate Gardens, my harmonica and my mouth's shore believing into be a map for migratory birds in lake Van rather in the Atlantic ocean

1.

Everybody looks for an acquaintance in this world
Looks for something white
and fills his album with the photos
of naked faces as many as he can find.
Photograph albums,
a shower of white visions: they will snatch our caps,
failing which, our heart.
I have always waited for April: what do I have to say
for pomegranate gardens
through which I passed leaving behind a jacket in tatters,
let me know.
What has remained to me other than the birds that
died after striking against my blue vest?
Let me know!
Whichever train I touch
the breath of cities in my palm
Whichever tree I embrace: autumnal occupation...

Like
the tiny feet of a ballerina
rain drops ricochet on my hair;
you have all become my acquaintances in this poem
Be ready to disband
in front of a red rose!

2.

Morning that taught me
how to look at the sky
with girls who had leaked winds into my trousers.
My evening walks were
but a letter
scribbled with dangerous dialogues.
Blue were the municipal buses
that descended toward Konak
as though they took their flight like butterflies,
from the suburbs,
crammed with high school girls
who wore their
stockings below their knees.
I fell in love every morning
with a bus load of girls;
I always carried a cigarette package
about me like a jack knife,
I had become
a sailboat
in the white screen
of a motion-picture theater.

3.

Everybody looks for an acquaintance in this world,
looks for something white. Some
expects to see oceans; some
would not even know
what insects, meadows, quails are?
How can one transport a carnation to the world?
Daisy fields which are
the fair spies of autumn hanging from chirping of birds.
A dry sea it had once been
the Mediterranean
before it became a long kiss.

155

Everybody looks for an acquaintance in this world,
looks for something white.
No one tells his fellow being that he died;
no one takes off the hat of a dead man: he fears!
The public veil their faces;
they know their head will be cut off
if they talk more than necessary
He keeps mum!
The public crave for shopping in markets,
listen to bands,
dance at weddings,
dip their bread in their dish of dry beans
make pickles, vote and likes to break
an onion between his palms.
The public stands to attention!

The public is led to war,
However, you better meet each other,
not in wartime
but in this poem.

4.
I'm coming from far far away. Hanging onto trains and
stars
taking each tree I pass by for my terminal
and taking
the children playing in the plateaus and torn clouds.
for my child.
These children! So lonely they are! Sorrows get broken
in their hands like a jug,
those sorrows have not been named yet.

Life I have been thrust into
with my salty and brown skin.

My life, O! my lion!
Illegal carnations I pinned on my lapel
are not enough to arouse God;
God!s shadow
is swifter than of us all! Man's shadow is so sof
that you could break it into two halves like a loaf of
bread

No witness to bear testimony to the great poem.
Cities are crammed with clowns and prompters
oral sex,
big size poetry anthologies
informatics
chips are victorious. Sodomy
is measured in megahertz.

Good morning dear little world of ours
Good morning, men, insects, birds and all the living
beings
Good morning nature!
The poetry bears testimony to you all
Look! The autumn is waiting for us
in a castle hooked on
the chirping of birds.
lip to lip with ants
Do you know by chance why the penis of the ants
is red? Why on earth
Lake Sapanca
gets cracked like a vase
once it is in this poem?

5.
Look I'm repeating once again. No one recognizes
anyone,

157

even in starry nights.
You don't recognize the mother of the baby
whose throat was cut
in Algiers.
How tacit you are dawn!
How long do you think
errors can protect you?
Don't forget! One day we'll turn back
naming the murders one by one
The dead
will be looking for their murderers
having come back to the Earth through
the holes that black tulips have drilled.

6.
I'm coming from far far away,
tired of measuring the dreams we dreamt.
carrying on my shoulder like a cross
the horizon line.
The scars of whips and rocks on my skin,
are not enough to arouse God.
Life and death
have changed their lips
are looking now for new ones. Who knows what?
Birds that drink water from the river.
do not know they are drinking from a mirror.
All colors, sounds and perfumes I wear
that tear off this can in order to pop up,
perch on my shoulders like shrieks of tenors.
The tree does not know
that it is a tree
that water is water
and the stone is a stone.
Nature never completes itself;

we are running on
from a dried river bed.
I'm ready now to fly
the naked hours of the morning.
Morning is surely
the most charming bomb
that rolls over the meadows.
the best damson plum
hanging toward the Earth on its branch?
Oceans , fish
and winds adjust the hour...
Solvents, cold metals
decayed plants and us that have dripped down
from that big foam.
We! We are a kite
hooked on stars; those stars
that on certain nights
furtively
steal down
to kiss the most beautiful girls

to appear to us more brilliant and sparkling
No matter how bright the stars may be
neither heartaches will cease
nor the spleen of trees will vanish; songs
will resound in the air.

"If you don't give me a kiss
I'll throw myself down from the
Eiffel Tower"

7.
I'm coming from far far away
I have been carrying the words from rivers

flowing through granites…
Behind me Route 66 and the Baghdad Café
I gave a name to everything: a house
should know that it is a house
Fields of poppy
should not think that they are a vast red ocean;
but I failed
to persuade my hands
that they were not canaries.
Every poem hides angels in it. With their white wings
they fly about among the words
The letter they dread is 'S'
For they believe they are flying in a dark tunnel.
They take 'O' for a dancing floor
and dance on it.
While 'I' is a space bus
to take them home.

8.
You can draw everything toward you, a cloud, a
sparrow, a township
You can have them in front of your door.
Last night you witnessed that the Taurus Mountains
were making love to a bay.
Just multiply the Chinese pornography
by the wall calendar
and sprinkle on it some Hungarian spleen
you'll end up directly in Rome.
But you cannot go through this poem
Not everybody
can go through a poem.
One can not alight at Taksim from every car one has
taken.
Come on, your gondola is waiting for you at the canal:

160

You are invited to a soirée of Liszt
You can move everything toward you except your heart!
For everybody has had its share of a single heart,
not permitted to be moved away.
If a pigeon has perched on your lapel
washed under the rays of the evening sun,
Your heart would have become a vagabond already
and in a yellow streetcar at Amsterdam
or a dark green field at the Black Sea region

Please record it in your diary
You will be passing through 2000
as you drink your cup of tea.

9.

I'm coming from far far away:
on the right of my white shirt
is the murdered Black Sea,
and, on the other, Route 66:
Jack Kerouac, J.D. Salinger
and John Steinbeck's Road to Freedom
The dusty road that carried the procession of peasants
from Oklahoma is remembered now only in songs.
Get your kicks on Route 66.
Deserted cities; Baghdad,
Arizona, Oatman, Marianne Segebrecht
had flown through a young tornado to the sky.
The motel is not closed yet: Blue Swallow
and a café whose door is a Cadillac.
bears a notice:
"Sorry we're open."
at the restaurant of Joe the Cactus
you may help yourself to a snake sandwich
and listen to Nat King Cole.

Route 66
Surmounted by Kerouac's cap
And Cadillac deaths
waiting for a bus
in front of
the Pacific.

10.
Everybody looks for an acquaintance in the world,
looks for something white... a white
township, perhaps;
stuck on the shore as a stamp. The horizon line
hangs like an electric wire
on a wharf;
bear like men with long white drawers
take a tumble in the sea.
The women,
with their naked feet, lost
in their plastic slippers
are busy looking for themselves.
Whenever a poem is recited
the villagers think that the township is on fire.
What they like most are drugstores.
They buy drugs by the kilo.

A township is represented by ugly constructions,
inexpensive markets, newly built mosques
and drugstores. Everybody
vies with each other to become
an unimportant person while he makes
as though he were an important person.
Everybody says everybody the same thing.
In a township nobody looks for an acquaintance;
Everybody is everybody else's acquaintance by birth

Yet nobody knows nobody.
Everybody conceals his heart as a secret from everybody
He shows the jack knife in his pocket
This is the reason why
no poem is composed in the township.
The township may be saved if ever,
by girls with newly budding breasts.

11.
I'm coming from far far away. Having borrowed
the wings of an angel.
in order to fly over Lake Van,
I stretched on the ground my red pelerine
in order to ask the queen of mountains
the favor of a dance.
I combed her hair
with the pigeons
perched on the shoreline of my mouth
having taken it for a migration map. I composed
This poem by wetting every word on your lips.
If this be our offense, my Queen!

Our defense
is your
magnificent beauty.

Dawn Bulletin

The most beautiful among gods is love
Jaroslav Seifert

1.
Dawn broke early this morning;
it gently swept away its violet hat in the wind
over the laced mountains
and snow-covered valleys.
The public who had learned to write letters
and to use weapons
from films,
celebrated their new year;
with a secret code
January's exposure for the world.

Your passes please!
said the ticket controller,
the girl students show
the first love letters.
The first love letters that were
the nostalgic flowers
of future loves
containing in them wells of spleen!
While I had been drinking
a green liquor stronger than raki
watching the flakes of snow.

That must be the reason why
I missed
the new year pigeons fly
piercing fly my palms
What will you be doing in the New Year's Eve.
I advise to you to better dance;
in dancing you can kill neither each other

nor any poems
Or you might powder your heart!
For not everyone's heart
is beautiful.

Everybody has not loved the red fish
in his childhood,
has not killed sparrows with a sling,
has not had calf-love at the primary school.

What is still more important,
no one has seen the world through
words.
One thing is certain though they must have traveled in a
phaeton
and wrote letters. As a matter of fact
the address of the letters and the phaeton
are written on them. Yet no one knows
their ultimate destination..
They are as long as a river.

I am very curious to know
about the number of horses required
to prevent a phaeton from falling into the sea,
about the number of poems that must be recited
in order to put an end to wars.

As a matter of fact man fights because of his ignorance.

Life is
as fugitive as the rays of the sun penetrating through
branches
as short as the steps of an ant.

Ask yourself. What have I done upon the Earth?

To how many poor you've stretched your hand?
How much did you love?
How much had your heart been ablaze with love?

2.
Dawn broke early this morning;
it gently swept away its violet hat in the wind
over the laced mountains
and snow-covered valleys.
The Salt Lake
asleep adjacent to heaven
broke out like a rose champagne
when it realized that it was the New Year.
A street-car in Los Angeles
was arrested
on charge of harassment
in the streets through which it passed.
Did you forget the great number of girls
who had harassed
Elvis Priestley?
The judge had brought restrictions to Elvis's
swaying of hips
to prevent its emulation
by his audience
as it might create too much
stir in the world.
But the rock and roll has gained immortality.
everybody was in perplexity that suited best his shrieks

3.
Everybody has a photograph
but angels' photographs are innumerable. Yet,
angels never get photographed,
nor do they ever drink tea with us.
They don't even have telephone numbers in the
directory.
Even though they're invisible to us,
their immediate presence is undeniable.
They fly about hovering above us.
So much so in fact, that I heard that between the lines of
my verses
they seemed to be riding in street-cars.

Angels are not counted in the world census.

Earth! Which had once been a crystal globe
you are remembered for your world tours
organized on board of cruises
aboard ships made of sedges and bamboos
the bubbling lava flowing down the heights
form the contents of library books
as though they were works of art now.

We have come down from Gargantuan highlands
and are heading for Lilliputian lowlands.
The weights of our shadows
are exactly the same.
Certain days they dwindle so much that
no matter where you go
You come back to the same place.

Our age's only free phenomenon
are winds that embrace us.

Learn how to embrace the winds!

4.

Dawn broke early this morning;
it gently swept away its violet hat in the wind
over the laced mountains
and snow-covered valleys.
And you entered the New Year
but you have not noticed that the moon
was watching you
like a daisy
What color is our world?
Are you aware that it changes its hue every second?
Can you recognize
the stardust showering on your jacket?

Go to the airport and take a plane;
Airports are the most organized
abysses of a city;
they are mass suicide attempts
in a mass of steel.
You may purchase now
perfumes, chocolates and drinks at reduced prices
from long legged hostesses
that have completed their course of eloquence.
Go and dance in discotheques
made of lemon and orange gardens!

I advise you not to drink raki while playing golf
the ball being of raki color
will be in a puzzle which hole to fall into
To my mind the best thing is clotted cream
only then will your face
be buried in dawn.

Beware not to close your eyes when you die;
otherwise you cannot see the angels
that have gathered around your head.
Angles are stark naked only when we die.

Happy New Year!

5.
Dawn broke early this morning;
it gently swept away its violet hat in the wind
over the laced mountains
and snow-covered valleys.
In Venice
birds' throbbing heart woke me up.
Why our living space is restricted to this world, I
thought.
Why our brethren from the space above
do not bring us presents.
I, for my part, would have liked to receive two stars
as radiant as the eyes of a maiden
to compose poems under their light;
or a space bicycle to ride among meteors;
but no matter where we go
we'll get caught by the dawn

Dawn is omnipresent!

I'am Not Clever Enough To Exchange Kisses With A Dynamite In My Mouth

1.
Bring me face to face with the new born day
unbutton my shirt
and throw it to the wind!
For, news came; that life has accepted me!
I'll spend some time more in life
in the company of fishes and trees;
Trees, our handsomest face.
Otherwise I'll be taken to task
for having failed to show men
what they had not seen.

The mountains! There they are!
The street, embracing a pigeon
in the most naked hour of the morning
I wish I had not informed you about the children
who showed the day in its most resplendent attire.
I wish I had not told you about
the world beauties
known to the ice-cream sellers in collapsed summer
cities.
Their hips are but small oceans
whose unruly billows
strike against the sun. I wish I had not told you
about Keriman Halis
but she was a reflection of the universe
This is the reason why I keep silent.

2.

But people misinterpreted my silence.
The yellow roses I had grown in my garden
have all been hand-cuffed.
When birds emerged
from the tulip bulbs I had planted in the earth,
the gendarmes took me away.

What's there to be afraid of
in the embracing of a pigeon
with the morning? I don't understand.
Why should one be afraid of the breath of a mare
whose teeth smell of fresh grass?
Everybody's life passes through everybody. Even the
Leander's Tower;
Who sometimes when it takes itself for a watchtower
bends toward the waters of the Bosphorus,
Üsküdar in its vest,
and turns into a scorpion, and indicates the time.
In fact, what it indicates is not time,
but an album of a devastated life.

3.

I, whose species is about to be extinct upon the Earth,
have not been able to choose a life style for myself.
I have identified a child's life
with my life.
I was not afraid to see
that the cherry tree had put on my shirt.
I have tossed my life
to other people's lives.
I have tossed my skin
toward other skins
I have learned how to shake off my life

along with the lives of others
I don't want to face it anymore. Kiss me, kiss me hard!
And let all the tickets in my pocket
become null and void.
You may tear my pocket off' if you like.
You may sew a cloud instead!
Let my swagger be set at naught.
To swagger in the presence of life and love is a delicate
affair.
Not comparable to having oneself photographed on the
Alps.
It is something like
the betrothal of Albatrosses with
abysses....

I don't know how to get engaged
But with words
I can adjust the time of the world.

I am not clever enough
To exchange kisses with a dynamite in my mouth

Allusions From The Lightness Of Intolerance Winter Of Collapsed Summer Townships To a Verdant Branch Floating on the Nile

1.

By joining the swallows in flight
I might have hidden myself
I might have asked your pardon
through breakfasts, a sign of my existence.
But how am I to ask forgiveness from the world?
From the townships that blemished me
in a dirty collaboration with
southerly winds.
In those townships
peasants stick behind their ears
a marigold instead of a cigarette.
They take their stands in the open markets
with their coca cola bottles filled with olive oils.
and with black grapes. When
the southerly winds begin to blow
in streets emitting hissing sounds
reminiscing the sound of a rock thrown by a sling,
there starts the lightness of the intolerable lightness of
winters;
there the promontory Karaburun!
I have always wondered who may have been
the person that planted it
on the shrieks of the seagulls.

Who lights the stars every night? I don't know.
I
Know
nothing
in fact!
I wonder why
the stark naked feet

of Arab maidens in black attire
perch upon my shirt like a pair of butterflies?
I wonder if
to drink raki with pickles juice
at the tavern of Ismet on the New Year's eve is like
shaking hands with a stark naked angel?

The only thing I am sure of in the world
is to get engaged to birds and townships.
Can one call that a ring the ring on my finger...
Riddled with holes are

Words
or
Lemon orchards

2.
By joining the swallows in flight
I might have hidden myself,
I might have asked your pardon
through breakfasts, a sign of my existence.
But how am I to ask forgiveness from the world?
How can one ask forgiveness
like a swaggering boy
from a township
that have just learned how to shake itself off?
April may have come to an early end!
We may have imperfectly looked at the mountains,
imperfectly exchanged kisses
with the winds and the maiden

What is imperfection, always in need for completion?
Where can love take us?
This would be something like
asking an aircraft that is about to crash

at what time
will it be landing at the Istanbul airport.

A verdant branch glanced at its watch:
What time is it?
What was the exact hour
at which the pyramids had been completed?
The cigar in my mouth,
the umpteenth cigar
that the Cuban women roll between their breasts.
Once I had addressed Cemal as Süreyya
"To hell with your Cemals and Süreyyas
Cut for me a slice of apple, will you?
Let one side have a subdued light
the other juicy
like Cleopatra's pussy.

3.
Today is Saturday
It may be a Sunday for all that; for
We misunderstand the days;
everything is misunderstood.
My falling in love with girls,
that had seen swallows fly from their camps
was misunderstood. They had thought
I came from the film industry
To meet them at deserted spots.

But please tell me
Is İzmir sparsely populated;?
You may not be visible, may you, in taxis you hail in
Ankara?
Whichever park of Stockholm you may wander into
you cannot avoid stepping over
the naked girls basking in the sun on the lawn

175

I have been too much around in the world!
The only place where we cut a figure is the world, any
way!
We shall not be appearing in anywhere else.
We are in nowhere else.

4.
By joining the swallows in flight
I might have hidden myself
I might have asked your pardon
through breakfasts, a sign of my existence.
but I who have been made famous
riding the words
growing toward the world
and my skin
which I rubbed with tangerine peels
seem to be too much involved in the world.
We have been tossed to and fro
nobody will believe us anymore
Woe to you! Woe to us!

Wherever I went
I was confronted with the Universe
O Universe, I said, O life!
Many thanks to you!
for the mussels
I had broken between my palms
for the young breasts
that I pressed
on my face.

I Was A Goal Keeper I The Junior High School

1.
What am I doing seated here?
I'd rather go to my garden to play with leopards.
I might just as well open a bar in Thailand for that
matter.
I'd sell smart Mediterranean blues.
Will you please pull aside
the lilac vapor on your lips and
make way for me dear.

2.
The fact I had been shut in prison in Bangkok
having first spilled my shirt into a red ocean
is not a conclusive evidence to prove my skin's guilt.
The skin has no consciousness;
It just disperses in different directions.

3.
I have put marks on the map
to indicate my secret love affairs
as pigeon nests; visible by no one.
Who sees anything anyway?
What's the name of the sky this morning?
Where can one hear the first word
that the budding lavender utters?
Where do *you* happen to be?

4.
Regardless of the horses I have caused to gallop
my hair has always clashed with the clouds.
I was always seen under that sky;
how often,
only goodness knows.

They have recognized me from the glitter on my lips,
a vestige of the salted and lemoned tequila.
So what? Let them recognize me.
Anyhow there remains something not known to
everybody:
I was a goal keeper in junior high school;
In February I usually defect to Thailand to become a
Buddhist
I learn how to become
a brother
to all the living creatures.

5.
May be I am a sailor,
who hardly knows to knot a necktie,
whose face reflects the Mediterranean blue
in ever-young evenings.
They call me: Sailor! Sailor!
How are going to pay back the spleens,
you have borrowed?

-If I am in default
I might give you instead
the birds decorating the edges of my notebook.

6.
Among us, it was Turgut Uyar who had used
the word 'TAILOR'
with the best skill.
On the other hand, I know best the address
of the river beds. I used to
put questions beautifully at the primary school.

-Why birds and villagers are brothers?
(Or aren't they?)

-Suppose you scratch your penis,
the State will immediately intervene: why?
(Omit this question since
everybody knows its answer)
-Is every township
a truck loaded with images?
(if not, why?)
Everybody thinks that he knows something,
but does not know what he knows.

7.
What a distance have we not covered!
Where are we heading for?
Anything new
under this canopy?

Don't tell me angels do not exist!

8.
I'd better go to my garden to play with leopards.
My beloved is preparing rice
stark naked in the kitchen.
Not even to her did I say that I had been
a goal keeper in the junior high school

That's why my heart has always been windy
You know what,

I don't believe any more in my heart!

On Monday's I'am From The World

1.

I have had my breakfast!
My face is nearer now to the world.
I am wearing a snow-white shirt with starched collars;
I have inaugurated my heart. It's true,
my heart has quite often been deceived,
by nature and by love in particular.
That's why my life
shall remain in embrace
with a mountain.

I'm entering a city
concealing the scratches
on my skin
I had traced with oysters.
The bourgeois, who walk with newspapers
and flowers in their hands
do not see me.

For today is Monday
and on Mondays I'm absent from the world.

We suddenly exist
We are suddenly extinct.
Suddenly love
Suddenly spleen

Suddenly minerals we become

2.

I have had my breakfast!
My face is nearer now to the world.
On my head a hat color of rainbow
getting ready for the conclusion of a love
Quite probably this will be my end
What have I done before my end?
I got on a red street-car in İstanbul
and got off at the Amik plain
then I realized I was in Antioch;
Full moon in the middle of the sky
from whose edge hung down
A small field of lettuce.
about to fall down into the Asi river
What if it does fall?
Not all the street-cars and the birds will fall into it surely.
This may be the reason, however
the river Asi
flows in the reverse direction
L e t   i t   f l o w!
I'd go out into balconies and terraces
redolent with medlar odors.
You'll see me there.
Perhaps not though; since it will be a Monday;
and I'm absent on Mondays from the world.
But if one day
you happen to see a heart
on the beak of an albatross... It's me
my own heart.
We suddenly exist
We are suddenly extinct.
Suddenly love
Suddenly spleen

Suddenly minerals we become

3.
I have had my breakfast!
My face is nearer now to the world.
My hair got entangled in the field of lettuce under the
full moon.
What sort of a life is this?
What sort of a love is this ?
I who have known so many loves
My heart is like an album
full of dangerous experiences.
All the birds from Mardin can bear testimony to this.

Why does this love never come to an end?
Could it be possible that I forgot how to put an end to
love?
Am I not the architect
of the word 'Separation'?

4.
I have had faith in birds and abysses
more than in human beings
To dodge any clash
I hung on words
and on poppy fields
No! No!
No matter how firmly I hung on words
This love will come to an end
and I will die.

I'll turn into a mass of marquis
on the skirt of the Mediterranean mountains
or perhaps a river
with its mineral waters in a forest

that has changed its course
puzzled which direction to take.

But Mondays excluded. For,
I'm absent on Mondays from the world.

I Have No Time To Learn What Life Is

I struck life with the wings of an albatross
I grew up along with lives I had been made to share
My skin got bruised on rose scented skins.
There's no mountain I haven't exchanged kisses with;
There's no ocean I haven't made love to.
As I grew up
my knowledge dwindled more and more.
I got it, life was a blue river flowing toward eternity.
Whereas I was a tiny ant on it.
I had no time to learn what life is
I may get drowned in it though.
I studied, I ran, Life has washed me.
I made scratches like a child on all the meadows, all the
cities
and all the clouds with words ...
I attached colorful balloons at the extremities.
I suddenly realized that a little bud
knew much more than I did.
The smell of the pebbles
I picked up upon the shore
Went back to millennia.
While I am but a bird
caught red-handed while fornicating with cherry trees
I have no time to learn what life is;
only rent asunder by a long kiss
can I die before it.
My blood will shower down over the mountains
Like red warm tropical rains
The mountains know me full well
The mountains know well what I say.

Poppy

1.

In the primary school I was at the head of those
who approached their hearts to poppies.
At the time Konya was the Konya of today; except for the
faces of dervishes;
whirling in the space; it was a black and white
photograph; for their faces and feet
had been kneaded with poppy petals, to enable them to
whirl better.

2.

No matter which street, which park I hit against, I
received no injury;
for whatever hit me became a white cloud automatically
This is the reason why the parks and the streets of İzmir
are so soft
Izmir is the stardust that falls every night from the space
onto the world!

3.

I was a curious child at school, and used to stick my
finger into every hole.
They had expelled me from the Koran course just
because I wanted to know
the why and wherefore of everything
Please Sir, why a dinosaur cannot fly any more?
Are fish our elder brothers?
Why poppies are at large every Saturday?

4.

The smallest mosque of the world is at Bitez, overlooking
the sea like a headgear
I stole it furtively in the night as though I was stealing a
sugar candy from a confectioner.

Had I been caught would God have looked askance at
me?

-And turn me into an orange garden?

5.

It would be marvelous! All the orange gardens my
brethren!
The tangerine gardens my beloved and the pomegranate
gardens my paramour.
But you know it, the poppy fields are no gardens but a
knife
thrown from the outer space
down upon the Earth.

6.

I don't know when I was first made part of the world
population.
It may be when I had been riding a horse on the Atlas
Mountains
One thing is certain though; the fact I had been stolen
from another planet
I had been thrown into the world concealed among the
petals of a poppy.

7.

My father was a blonde cavalry sergeant. He often
frequented our house,
Over long years, but I saw neither his face nor his horse.
They did not even inform me of his decease
He had two brothers, world champions in wrestling in
the 50s.
When they brought their rivals' backs on the ground out
came sparkles of fire

186

Then they saluted the audience with poppies behind
their ears.

8.

The person I loved most was my mother, a slim brunette;
With brown luminous eyes. A Miss Aegean and Miss
World
When she kissed me my hair reached to the clouds
She held me by the hand to show the poppy field.

This must be the reason why
girls with luminous brown eyes have always fascinated
me.

And poppies of course.

Whatever Happens Happen In This World

1.
Summer again! I am being tracked by its detectives,
who take the picture of every flower I smell
Let it do so! I will jump over those magnificent and
endless blues
in the company of the Beydağları Mountains
The Taurus Mountains will then bear us testimony.

O the big blue summer! If you so wish
you may shoot us along with the maquis;
if you cannot do so, than you blue us!

2.
I passed by riding my red bicycle
by the collapsed summer townships
who take themselves for tourism paradise
in my lap my beloved with loose sleeves.

There! A street declared Miss Universe!
One extremity hanging down from an orange garden,
the other about to fall into the sea,
The address : İnci Sokak, Bodrum.

Whenever my heart is spilled onto the world
I ask my face from the streets
the most frequented by birds
For in those streets have I lost my youth.

But Only I know İzmir best;
for, those who have come from far will know
best the smell of those houses

All right? What's your occupation Mr Şükrü?

-I am a migrant worker and drink raki

3.

There's always something missing in the world. Nobody
knows what exactly.
The starlings that steal the first rays of the morning,
the fig tree darting in through my window...

At what hour exactly ends the best love?
Why do the heartaches have no passport?

Whatever happens happens in this world
I am hugging you in this world darling;
flowers blossom in this world;
the sun rises in this world.

There's no other world!

4.

Everything is equal to something but death is equal to
itself.

5.

A city plus a love
plus a street
plus stars
divided by chrysanthemums
is equal to what?
Poetry is not a table of multiplication, you will say.
If not, what is it then?
Is it the people that cram the blue private buses?

Come on, stop the bus and ask:
-O public! O great public
When did you ever touch the world?
Where are you?
Where is your voice?
Where is your face?

Oratorio Of Children Grown Up Without Any Idea Of May

1

O children who are grown up without any idea of May!
I say to you: Don't ever believe
in catamarans and daisies,
Take your hands off from the early mourning,

Don't get stuck on your childishness at your first shot
like kites caught by branches of trees.
Know your body well.
Let everything be your photograph

Manacle your heartaches using an apple garden as
handcuffs
and let your sorrows be your compass
Neither love nor sorrow is enough for the world
ask yourself : are we late?

No, you're not!
for you are in a rose's mouth
for your are very near May.
You! You did what you'd been told.

2.

O children grown up without any idea of May,
young men with dark blue voices, blue skinned girls
you asked for very beautiful things
from abysses you kept on your faces.

You had been a boy scout in the primary school beating
drums, did you forget it?
Three times tap tap, tap tapa tap, tap tapa tap tap

With your pocket knife and whistle your childhood
deceived you;
you changed the order of the streets

With your pencil with a soft tip
you drew birds on the edge decorations,
all gone now;
that's why you have no diaries.

The girls you loved decorated the beds of greasy
guttersnipes;
fertilized over and over again before being thrown aside
They are now plump women with a host of children
that fill their bags in open market

Nothing to fear!
Everything goes fine. We have even metrosexual
muezzins
with golden earrings
we have become eligible now for EU membership.

3.
O children grown up without any idea of May
I say to you: everything is made transitory
a lifetime is difficult to define
but I ask you

Have you
Ever watched
the stars
at night
from
a
Yörük tent?

I Have A Degree Rewarded For Flying The Most Beautiful Birds Over The Rivers

1.
I am alone at last.
I came through meridians and the blue deltas
My arms may not be as fire resistant as asbestos
But I have a degree awarded
for flying the most beautiful birds over the rivers.

I am an eternal fugitive like nature itself.

2.
I study my childhood in my quiet corner.
I am condemned
to carry in my heart the blue frost
Although I am an incorrigible fugitive,
I am the last witness of the orchids

My life passes through other lives.

3.
Three different words, of course: Tibet, Warsaw and
Gümüşhane.
The cleanest is Palandöken, for it is washed by dawn
every morn.
Why do the 'fairy chimneys' not take off their hats at
Cappadocia?
I have seen he sunset at the Ihlara Valley.

Splendid and smuggled things will be my end.

4.
I am alone at last, I see and I hear everything.
All the words and the hearts have discharged their
contents.
193

A stench comes from the decaying cell
A country whose internal bleeding never ceases!

The dirtiest word: The Power!

Life Is My Most Beautiful Sin

I am ready to blow up everything
I am ready to mark all the ports
even though my undershirt is torn by a shooting star
Nobody is responsible for my wounds.

For I have been clashing using words as weapons.
I have been embroidered with the peoples of the world.
I got on board and watched the universe

Whatever I saw I sent it to you loaded on an Albatross's
wings

Glance at your watch: It's April
The month in which water is bluest that runs from the
fountains of the village.
The abyss into which I dived with its wick aflame in my
mouth.

No matter how much I am kissed the hiccup remains in
my throat.

Are all the birds from Mardin and roses my diary?
Have I learned how to watch the mountains? No!
There is something certain, however!
Streams and the rose spleen will affect me always:

For life is my most beautiful sin.

Today I Made Love To An Octopus

1
I had my breakfast today at Gümüşlük
spreading the blue of the sea spilled on my slice of bread.

Life began with my wild mouth.

I became a hollow bamboo through which I let pass the
world.
O the number of flowers, of abysses, of rivers
of people and of insects in your house, O God!
to live is to conceive you in a sense.

2.
I had my breakfast today at Gümüşlük
I painted my face with the spilled blues of the sea
I've become the sea.! I've become the wave! I've become
the bird!
I breathed with the entire universe!

With whom do angels dance in Paradise?
What do I care who are scorched in hell!

Everything is now and everything is a miracle

3
I had my breakfast today at Gümüşlük
Having collected the spilled blues of the sea
Offered them as a wreath to the Leleg
in the engulfed millennia old Myndos city

We poured into our glasses
Red wine and eucalyptus whistles

4.
Everything creates its own form
Albatrosses are albatrosses, oceans oceans…

But you are everything! Cleanse yourself and join life!
Don't be a clothes-peg,
be rater a passage! Be water and flow!

Let your heart hang from the heights,
be the daughter or the son
of the planet on which you live

And while you leave the world
see to it that you have not polluted it!

5.
Tonight I flirted with stars at Gümüşlük
Sirius The most coquette wanted to have the favor of a
dance.
my neck bears the traces of its kisses.
In the sky a huge moon like a lemon
watches us with envy. On it a little girl riding her bicycle
is waving her hand to us.

Everything exists this moment and everything is a
miracle
To live is like conceiving God.

Look!
I am making love with an octopus at Gümüşlük!

I Learned How To Read My Body

1.
I learned how to read my body
and to touch the Earth.

I learned the triangles,
how to sit in the angles of a triangle;
and jump to the mountains from its flanks.
I put my trust in the mountains and triangles

If I have been deceived, a bean shoot deceived me,
trees have deceived me,
poppies and poetry deceived me.

The little islands in the midst of oceans
have deceived me.

The more I was deceived the more grew up
have been deceived by
nature love words

but never deceived by humans.

2.
I learned how to read my body
how to touch the Earth and
everything I was curious about. Where
do they bury the stars when they die?
If Lake Titica is a kite
fallen on the mountains?
Whose heart is Peru?

Perhaps I am a magician; the entire ocean
would not be large enough for me.
But if you dye my vest with three oceans

I can spurt even birds from their lining.

3.
I learned how to read my body
how to touch the Earth

I am conscious of life.

You!
Ever Been A Star And Watched The Earth

I have never believed in
islands, seagulls and tailors
swinging like a swing
in the midst of the ocean

The islands,
are abysses when the stars
appear brightest in the night
now and then shifting their places
with our hearts.

You!
Ever been a star and watched the Earth?

Those seagulls that paste the collapsed summer
townships
they carry on their wings
on the world map.

The tailors come with their huge pairs of scissors
and sew
costumes
and uniforms that fit their customers

Ask yourselves:
-who are you?
-Who have you been?

I trusted in the bougainvillea the most;
but I have never witnessed the bougainvillea
quit the table with a single shot;
at their third shots they
find themselves buried

200

in Kars.

You may also see them
transformed into a red street-car
in Istanbul
at the back of which children
hook on.

Whistle Of The Universe

1.

O the things I've stolen from the world
the morn is what becomes most to my face
strewn with shrieks of albatrosses!

No matter how masked may
my acquaintance be with oceans and cities
I'm no stranger to the world, as they know me
by the hat I wear.

What I wear is actually
the Fethiye blue!

My tanned face has mixed up time with fire and roses
that must be the reason why I failed to find the address
of my house.
a house I have never owned! For my wounds and the
odor of the steppe
have been my house

Astride on the winds
I have pursued an odor

The summer has come to a close
catamarans, ice-cream sellers
and tanned women are no more, alas!

The summer has come to a close,
the guests of resorts
went away leaving their pets to perish
and their garbage and tittle-tattles.

The month of July is almost in;
the time I allow it
to fondle my private parts;
so are birds, insects and trees ,
the whole nature in fact.
The public that received the severest blow
hardly recognize their own faces
their hands and hearts
they themselves in fact.

The public is streaming
Humanity is streaming.

2.

O the things I've stolen from the world: for instance
Gümüşlük was as beautiful as a leopard's misty eyes.
The place where love is consumed
between the sun and the human beings.

The summer has come to a close!
Vacant deck-chairs staring at the sky
with blank looks filled with dejection

A crazy red has just emerged from the blue

A fisherman pulls his oars in the sea
I do the same with my heart that lands at a coastal
village
waiting for the almond trees to blossom.

I am as drunken as the clouds
that have strayed from their course and ended up
towering the world.

I am a Badawi with naked feet

looking for a way out in the scorching deserts

No I am not guided by the stars
but by the whistle of the universe.

PUBLİSHED BOOKS

*

BİR ELMA BÜYÜKLÜĞÜNDE SAKALLARIM
Şiir / ilk şiirler 1960

KURACAĞIZ HERŞEYİ YENİDEN :
Şiir/ / 1969 / DTCF Yay. / Ankara

IRGATOĞLU ATÇALI KEL MEHMET :
Destan /1970/ Yabanel yay. / Berlin

KIRLANGIÇLAR,KIRLANGIÇLAR :
Şiir /1978 /AR yay / Ankara

SANEM OKULA BAŞLIYOR :
Çocuk kitabı /1981 / Skriptor yay. / Stockholm

İŞTE HAYAT! İŞTE ÖLÜM VE TARİH! :
Şiir /1984 / Dayanışma Yay / Istanbul

STOCKHOL'DE MAVİ SAATLER :
Şiir / 1987 / Broy Yay / İstanbul

DÜNYA ÇARPIYOR YÜZÜME :
Toplu şiirler /1988 / CEM yay / İstanbul

MOZART VE AKDENİZ :
Şiir / 1992 / CEM Yay / İstanbul

BİR IRMAKLA DÜELLO EDİYORUM :
Şiir / 1995 / Oğlak yay / İstanbul

DİREN! EY KALBİM
Şiir kaseti/kendi sesinden / 1998 / Yeni Dünya Yay /
İstanbul

KENTLERİN SENFONİSİ :
Şiir / 2000 / BOYUT yay / İstanbul

VAN GÖLÜ SAVUNMASI :
Şiir / 2001 / Rotary yay / İzmit

NEHİR:
Toplu Şiirler /1960-2002/ BOYUT / İstanbul / 2002

BEN SAVAŞCI DEĞİL GÜL YETİŞTİRİCİYİM:
Seçme şiirler / Dünya yay / Akkor dizisi / 2005 /
İstanbul

GELİNCİKYA :
Şiir / Hayal / 2006

YERYÜZÜ ŞARKILARI :
Tüm Şiirleri 1960-2008 / 2008 Mayıs/ BOYUT Yayınları
/İstanbul

SOBEEE! :
Şiir / Ocak 2010 / Hayal yayınları

ÖZKAN MERT ARTSHOP ŞİİR DİZİSİ :
1.Bir elma büyüklüğünda sakallarım / 2.Kuracağız her
şeyi yeniden / 3.Irgatoğlu Atçalı Kel Mehmet
Destanı-Kırlangıçlar kırlangıçlar / 4.İşte hayat! İşte ölüm
ve Tarih! / Artshop Yay / Ekim 2009

ŞİİR ANTOLOJİLERİ:

SVENSKA KVINNORS KÄRLEKSDIKTER (İSVEÇLİ KADINLARIN AŞK ŞİİRLERİ ANTOLOJİSİ) Türkçe-İsveçce Podium Yay 1998 Stockkholm/ Papirus Yay.İstanbul 2003 / Artshop 2008 İstanbul

ÖVERSÄTT INTE ETT LEVANDE SPRÅK TILL ETT DÖTT (YAŞAYAN BİR DİLİ ÖLÜ BİR DİLE ÇEVİRME) 7 Dil'de GUNNAR EKELÖF / İsveçceden Türkçeye çeviri. 2005 / Svenska Institutet / İskenderiye

7 DİL'DEN, 7 İKLİMDEN ŞİİRLER : Dünya Şiir Antolojisi / 2008 Mayıs / artshop

GECE GÜNEŞİ / MIDNATTSOL Modern Iskandinav Şiir Antolojisi / Türkçe-İsveçce Aralık / 2014

HAKKINDA YAZILAN KİTAPLAR

A' DAN Z' YE ÖZKAN MERT ŞİİRİ Ersan Erçelik / Ekim 2009 / Artshop

İSVEÇCE YAYINLANAN ŞİİR KİTAPLARI:

KÄMPA MITT HJÄRTA (DİREN ! EY KALBİM) Şiir /1981 / Skriptor Yay / Stockholm

TANGO ÖVER EGEISKA HAVET (EGE DENİZİNDETANGO) Şiir kaseti /1990

İXILENS BLUES (SÜRGÜN EZGİLERİ)

207

Şiir / 1999 / Svartvitts Yay / Stockholm

FÖRSVARSTAL ÖVER VANSJÖN (VAN GÖLÜ
SAVUNMASI)
Şiir / Svartvitt Yay. 2003/

Ödülleri ve üyelikleri:

*Cumhuriyet Yunus Nadi M - 1990
*İlhan Demiraslan Şiir Büyük Ödülü-1990
*Salihli Şiir İkindileri Dianysos Şiir Ödülü-1990
*Petrol-İş Jüri Özel ödülü-1992
*Gölcük Rotary Hizmet Ödülü-2001
(Yılın en iyi şairi)
*Cemal Süreya Şiir Ödülü-2008.

*2012 Datça Can Yücel festivali Onur Konuğu
*2013 Bursa Dünya Şiir Günü Onur Ödülü
*Türk-Macar Derneği onur üyesi
*Rodos Yazarlar ve Çevirmenler Konseyi Yönetim
Kururlu Üyesi
*İsveç Yazarlar Sendikası üyesi.
*İsveç PEN kulübü 'Tutuklu yazarlar komitesi üyesi'
*Türkiye Yazarlar Sendikası üyesi.
* Türkiye Edebiyatçılar Derneği eski Başka yardımcosı.

www.ingramcontent.com/pod-product-compliance
Lightning Source LLC
Chambersburg PA
CBHW051958090426
42741CB00008B/1446